What people are saying about …

Unexplainable

"The wisdom God has given Don Cousins about life and ministry has been a tremendous help to me over the past fifteen years. Now it is distilled in the strongly biblical, practical, and concise book that you hold in your hands. I highly recommend it!"

Chip Ingram, author of *Overcoming Emotions That Destroy*, president and teaching pastor of Living on the Edge

"In this book, Don Cousins addresses our deep longings for genuine contentment, success, and significance. Most of us have difficulty bridging the gap between our longings and our realities. Only God can bridge that gap, and Don shows us how. Don explains the unexplainable work of God with such clarity and force that you'll immediately want more of it in your life. Don's is a wise and insightful voice informed by Scripture and seasoned by years of fruitful leadership in ministry. You will love this book!"

Rory Noland, director of Heart of the Artist Ministries and worship pastor at Harvest Bible Chapel

"Most of us are in hot pursuit of the valuable commodities of contentment, success, and significance. Our problem is not the pursuit—that's instinctive. It's that we are looking in all the wrong places. Don Cousins turns our hearts and head in the right direction and reveals God's plans for experiencing the joys of a life that has found the answers to our deepest dilemmas. This book is like having a divine GPS through the mysterious passages of life."

Dr. Joseph M. Stowell, president of Cornerstone University, Grand Rapids, Michigan

What people are saying about …

Don Cousins

"What Don Cousins writes, I read. He's among the most insightful church experts in the world. I know from personal experience the joy of being under his leadership."

Lee Strobel, author of *The Case for the Real Jesus*

"I've known Don for over thirty years. Without question he is blessed with one of the finest strategic ministry minds in America. I have deeply benefited from his mentoring and friendship."

Dan Webster, founder of Authentic Leadership, Inc.

"Don Cousins is by far one of the most effective communicators in the world. His profound insight, practicality, and relevance are the best."

Dan Chun, pastor of First Presbyterian
Church of Honolulu

UNEXPLAINABLE

Pursuing a Life Only God Can Make Possible

Don Cousins

David C Cook®
transforming lives together

UNEXPLAINABLE
Published by David C. Cook
4050 Lee Vance View
Colorado Springs, CO 80918 U.S.A.

David C. Cook Distribution Canada
55 Woodslee Avenue, Paris, Ontario, Canada N3L 3E5

David C. Cook U.K., Kingsway Communications
Eastbourne, East Sussex BN23 6NT, England

The Web site addresses recommended throughout this book are offered as a
resource to you. These Web sites are not intended in any way to be or imply an
endorsement on the part of David C. Cook, nor do we vouch for their content.

Unless otherwise indicated, Scripture quotations are from the *New American Standard
Bible* ©1960, 1977, 1995 by the Lockman Foundation. Used by permission.
Other Scripture quotations are from *The Holy Bible,* King James Version (KJV) The Holy
Bible, *English Standard Version* (ESV) © 2001 by Crossway Bibles, a division of Good News
Publishers. Used by permission. All rights reserved. *The Holy Bible,* New International
Version (NIV) ©1973, 1984 by International Bible Society, used by permission of Zondervan.
The author has added italics to Scripture quotations for emphasis.

LCCN 2009929975
ISBN 978-1-4347-6808-7
eISBN 978-0-7814-0353-5

© 2009 Don Cousins
Published in association with the literary agency of Wolgemuth & Associates, Inc.

The Team: Terry Behimer, Thomas Womack, Jaci Schneider, Karen Athen
Cover Design: Amy Kiechlin

Printed in Canada
First Edition 2009

1 2 3 4 5 6 7 8 9 10

062609

In memory of my father,
DONALD J. COUSINS,
who went home on September 27, 1990,
but whose influence lives on to this day, in and through me.
My ability to understand the unexplainable nature of God's grace
was made significantly easier by the grace I experienced
through this man I called Dad.

CONTENTS

Acknowledgments

There are a number of people I would like to recognize and thank for the role they played in the completion of this book. For each of them I say, "Thank You, Lord; I am blessed."

Thank you to the team at David C. Cook—namely, Terry Behimer, Don Pape, Jaci Schneider, Ryan Dunham, Mike Kennedy, Marilyn Largent, Ingrid Beck, Michelle Webb, Amy Kiechlin, Dan Rich and Cris Doornbos—all committed, capable, and a joy to work with.

Thank you to Thomas Womack, who loves God's Word and joyfully used his editorial abilities to improve upon my efforts.

Thank you to the team at Wolgemuth and Associates, who have stood with me since day one, and jumped in to assist wherever and whenever called upon.

Thank you to Nancy VanDyke, who once again typed out every handwritten page, and did so with the heart of a servant.

A special thanks to Dave and Cindy Siegers and Ed and Dimple Owens, who gave me the freedom to share their stories.

An extra special thank you to my wife, MaryAnn, who provided valuable insights that improved this manuscript in addition to the daily support that's so important; and to my three children, Kyle, Kirk, and Karalyne, who serve as daily reminders of God's unexplainable grace to me.

Most of all, I thank God for His grace which abounds in my life, and for the truth of His Word … which truly does set us free.

1

UNEXPLAINABLE ...
APART FROM GOD

"For My thoughts are not your thoughts, nor are your
ways My ways," declares the LORD. "For as the heavens
are higher than the earth, so are My ways higher than
your ways and My thoughts than your thoughts."

ISAIAH 55:8–9

God is beyond us—able to think and act in ways that defy human logic and surpass human understanding. He's limitless in power and He's infinite in knowledge, wisdom, and understanding.

For the sake of relationship, He lowers Himself to our level in many ways. Yet He often chooses to express Himself in ways that are, well, unexplainable—apart from Him. And He does this to point us *to* Him.

A Story of the Unexplainable

Abraham was seventy-five years old when God told him he would be the father of "a great nation." God instructed him to leave his relatives and his homeland and to venture out with his wife, Sarah, to a land that the Lord would show him, a land that would one day belong to his descendants. It was an incredible promise, an outrageous offer.

There was just one problem. Abraham and Sarah were childless. It's impossible to give land to descendants you don't have. It's equally impossible to father a nation when you haven't fathered a family. While Abraham and Sarah had certainly tried to bear children, it hadn't happened. And now, at the ages of seventy-five and sixty-five respectively, their chances of doing so were virtually nil.

Nonetheless, Abraham and Sarah, in obedience to the word of the Lord, left home in quest of this Promised Land and the birthing of a nation. They must have believed God would perform a miracle, enabling them to bear a child.

It wasn't long into their journey that they reached the territory God had for them. The Lord appeared to Abraham there and told him, "To your descendants I will give this land" (Gen. 12:7). Now all they needed were descendants to give this land to. But months passed, years passed—and still no child.

God reiterated His promise, telling Abraham, "One who will come forth from your own body, he shall be your heir" (15:4). In dramatic fashion God led Abraham outside at night. "Now look toward the heavens, and count the stars, if you are able to count them.… So shall your descendants be" (15:5).

However awesome this must have sounded to Abraham, Sarah remained barren.

Then one day, she had an idea. Abraham could bear a child by another woman—by Sarah's Egyptian maid, Hagar. Sarah had come to the logical conclusion that the Lord had "prevented" her from having children (16:2); it was no longer humanly possible for her. But Abraham could father a child by another woman.

This made sense to Abraham, so he had sexual relations with Hagar. Sure enough, she gave birth to a son, who was named Ishmael. Abraham was eighty-six when the boy was born (Gen. 16:16).

Laughable, but True

At this point, the Bible goes silent for thirteen years. When Abraham's story resumes, he's ninety-nine—some twenty-four years removed from the day God first issued the promise.

Once again He comes to Abraham and reiterates His promise more strongly than ever:

> I will multiply you exceedingly.... And you will be the father of a multitude of nations.... For I have made you the father of a multitude of nations. I will make you exceedingly fruitful, and I will make nations of you.... I will establish My covenant between Me and you and your descendants after you throughout their generations.... I will give to you and to your descendants after you, the land of your sojournings ... for an everlasting possession. (Gen. 17:2–8)

God also adds this about Sarah: "I will bless her, and indeed I will give you a son by her" (17:16).

How does Abraham respond? "Then Abraham fell on his face and laughed" (17:17). This was so ridiculous, so absurd, so inconceivable and incomprehensible, he couldn't help but laugh in God's face.

So Abraham offered God a suggestion—an alternative option that he and Sarah had hatched: "Oh that Ishmael might live before You!" (17:18). In other words, "What about the son I already have? Why not make him the first descendant? I'm not getting any younger, so let's get on with things!"

God's answer is direct and unmistakable: *"No"* (17:19). He tells Abraham, "Sarah your wife will bear you a son, and you shall call his name Isaac; and I will establish My covenant with him for an everlasting covenant for his descendants after him." Moreover, God promises that Sarah will give birth to this son within a year's time.

When this news reached Sarah's ears a short time later, she too laughed in the face of God (18:12).

But as you know, God's promise proved true. Abraham (at the age of one hundred) and Sarah (at ninety) did have a child, whom they named Isaac.

The Delay Explained

Why then did God have Sarah and Abraham wait so long—a quarter century—to see His promise fulfilled? Was He merely testing their willingness to obey? Was He wanting to stretch their faith?

I think the best answer to this question is found in God's response following Sarah's laughter: "Is anything too difficult for the LORD?" (18:14).

I believe God had them wait because He wanted to do that which could be explained only by *His* involvement—that which is *unexplainable apart from God.* In this way, the very life of Isaac and the fulfillment of the promise would point to God Himself. There could be no other explanation. Isaac was unexplainable—apart from God. Ishmael, on the other hand, was explainable: A man has sexual relations with a woman of childbearing age, and she gets pregnant. But when a baby's born to a century-old man and his wife of ninety after they've tried unsuccessfully for decades to have children—well, there's only one explanation for that: *God did it.* Isaac's very existence would always point to God. This is what God wanted, and it's why I believe He had Abraham and Sarah wait so long.

This is the sort of thing God desires to do in and through the lives of all His children. He wants to do the inconceivable, the uncommon, the unexpected, the remarkable, the incomprehensible, so that He—*God*—is the only explanation for what occurs in our lives. In this way, our lives point to Him.

Do you realize that God created you to point to Him? Do you understand that your life is intended to make Him known? God wants the unfolding of your life to be unexplainable apart from Him. As Paul expresses it, "We are His workmanship, created in Christ Jesus for good works, which God prepared beforehand so that we would walk in them" (Eph. 2:10). You've been created for good works that put God on display. Just as a work of art reflects the artist, we are to reflect God.

Jesus said it this way: "Let your light shine before men in such a way that they may see your good works, and *glorify your Father* who is in heaven" (Matt. 5:16).

His Ways Point to Him

If who you are, and the unfolding of your life, are seen as something understandable, expected, common, and explainable in human terms, then your life merely points to you. Like Frank Sinatra, you can sing, "I did it my way." But if the best and perhaps only explanation for your life is God, then you point to Him and your life plays to the lyric, "I did it His way."

This is the purpose for which you were created. In fact, to be unexplainable apart from God is completely normal for the Christian. This is the way life ought to be. You, and the unfolding of your life, should be unexplainable apart from God.

Perhaps in moments of quiet reflection you've wondered, *Is this all there is to life?* You have a sense within that there must be more to life than you're experiencing. Though you're probably busier than you want to be, you can't figure out why you're bored. You think there must be more to life than this.

Well, there is!

God is issuing an invitation to each and every one of us to join Him in the realm of the unexplainable. God wants to take your life *beyond you*. This is the kind of life He created you for, the life He designed you to experience. He wants it to be unexplainable apart from Him, so that you point to Him.

If you accept His invitation, then you join not only Abraham, Sarah, and Isaac, but a host of others, like:

- Joseph, who took an unexplainable-apart-from-God journey from a pit to a palace, then extended unexplainable-apart-from-God forgiveness to his brothers for the evil they did to him.

- Moses, who arrived unexplainably-apart-from-God at a palace, only to be exiled to the wilderness, where he was unknowingly being prepared to return to that palace—so he could lead God's people on an unexplainable-apart-from-God journey through that wilderness.

- David, who was such an unexplainable-apart-from-God choice to be Israel's next king that he wasn't even invited along with his brothers to the draft.

- Esther, who unexpectedly and unexplainably-apart-from-God "attained royalty for such a time as this," so that her people, God's people, could be saved from annihilation.

- Joseph and Mary, very common folk who were asked to do the most uncommon thing of all—give birth in an unexplainable-apart-from-God way to the very Son of God.

- Peter, James, John, and nine other young men from meager means and education who were chosen unexplainably-apart-from-God by Jesus to lead a movement that changed the world.

- A fellow named Saul, better known as Paul, who fought to wipe Christianity from the face of the earth, but unexplainably-apart-from-God ended up becoming Christianity's greatest ambassador.

The Bible is full of story after story of the "unexplainable apart from God." So true is this that skeptics have labeled the Bible as largely fairy tale and myth. They ask, "How can these things be?" God answers them as did Abraham: "Is anything too difficult for the LORD?"

For Superstars Only?

At this point you may be thinking, *But the Bible tells the stories of the superstars of the faith, and I'm no superstar.* While this is certainly a common perception, a closer look reveals that the vast majority of the Bible's primary figures were very common and ordinary folk. They were shepherds like Moses and David, or ranchers like Abraham, or fishermen like Peter, James, and John, or carpenters like Joseph in the New Testament. They were slaves like the Old Testament Joseph and Daniel, or tax collectors like Matthew and Zaccheus. Some were even prostitutes like Rahab, and social outcasts like Elijah, Jeremiah, and John the Baptist.

These people lived extraordinary lives, becoming the "superstars" we perceive them to be only as a result of following God's leading into the realm of the unexplainable. And this is what God desires to do with you as well. Common people become everything but common when God gets involved.

In most cases and on most days, the results of following God's guidance will not be dramatic. While we tend to focus on Daniel's dramatic rescue one night in the lion's den, what's even far more unexplainable is how Daniel chose earlier to continue "kneeling on his knees three times a day, praying and giving thanks before his God, as he had been doing previously" (Dan. 6:10), despite the king's edict that made such prayer a capital offense.

While we focus on David's unexplainable ability with a slingshot, it's even more unexplainable that for ten years he served faithfully under Saul, a king gone mad who even tried to kill David on numerous occasions. When the tables turned, and David had a chance to kill Saul, he refused to do so—a decision explainable only by God's influence in David's life.

Then there's Joseph, revered as the dreamer who rose from a pit to a palace. While his ascent is clearly unexplainable apart from God, it was Joseph's ability to forgive his brothers and to care abundantly for them and their families that truly defies the common and begs for explanation.

Following God into the realm of the unexplainable may produce some dramatic moments like those experienced by Daniel, David, and Joseph. In most cases, however, you'll find yourself living the unexplainable in the midst of very common circumstances and ordinary days. To embrace life in God, to experience His presence, and to follow His lead will inevitably place you in the realm of the unexplainable. You'll find yourself feeling, thinking, speaking, acting, and relating in ways leading unquestionably to the conclusion that "God did it." This is how it should be in every Christian's life.

Still True Today

Consider a couple who are friends of mine. They spent two years designing and building their dream home on five acres in a prestigious area, only to sell it four years after moving in because they felt led by God to give more of their resources to the cause of Christ and the poor in particular. Or another friend, a very successful executive, who took early retirement, thereby forfeiting significant financial gain, so he could follow God's leading into volunteer work with several ministries.

In both these cases, some asked, "What are you doing? Have you lost your mind? Your decision makes no sense." But these friends would tell you today that their decisions made total sense.

God may lead you to stay at a job in spite of a demanding and unreasonable boss—a decision that seems unexplainable when fellow employees are jumping ship.

God may lead you to pass up a promotion and all the perks that go with it, because of the additional hours and responsibilities that would negatively impact your family and current ministry involvements.

You may be led by God to write a check that will be unexplainable to your financial planner. This is exactly what the Macedonian Christians did, as Paul tells us: "For I testify that according to their ability, and *beyond their ability*, they gave of their own accord" (2 Cor. 8:3).

You may feel unexplainably prompted to share your faith in Jesus with a total stranger or with someone who previously made it clear he or she had no interest in God.

You may feel unexplainably compelled to befriend and express love to someone whom most others choose to avoid.

In other situations, God may choose to do the unexplainable on your behalf—like send His healing power upon your body to do what medical science has been unable to do, or bring reconciliation to a relationship you thought was beyond repair, or provide unexpected resources that ease your financial burden, or open a door to a job that's even better than the one you were hoping and praying for, or anoint a ministry involvement that ends up bearing more fruit than you thought possible.

Whatever it is, God wants to lead you into this realm of the "unexplainable apart from Him"—so your life points to Him.

Paul describes this new realm in these words: "Things which eye has not seen and ear has not heard, and which have not entered the heart of man, all that God has prepared for those who love Him" (1 Cor. 2:9). Wow! Count me in!

But How?

The question then becomes, *How do I get there?*

For this to happen, you'll need to see and approach life differently. Paul makes this truth abundantly clear when he commands our complete makeover in thought and behavior: "Do not be conformed to this world, but be transformed by the renewing of your mind, so that you may prove what the will of God is, that which is good and acceptable and perfect" (Rom. 12:2). Living in conformity to the world can't get you into this new realm. You'll need to undergo a transformation—one that begins with the "renewing of your mind" and results in conformity to the will of God.

This transformation from explainable to unexplainable is what this book is about. Specifically, I want to encourage and challenge you to make three major shifts in the way you see and approach life. I call them *lifeshifts*. They're the sort of thing I believe Paul had in mind when he told us to "not be conformed to this world, but be transformed by the renewing of your mind." These lifeshifts will dramatically alter the way we seek to fulfill three of the deepest longings of the human heart—contentment, success, and significance.

The first lifeshift is *from outside-in to inside-out*—and it opens the door to experiencing the kind of contentment that is unattainable and unexplainable apart from God.

So, if you're ready, turn the page … and begin your journey into the realm of the unexplainable.

Discussion Questions

1. What's your initial reaction to this book's fundamental premise—that you and the unfolding of your life should be in some ways unexplainable apart from God?

2. To what degree do you want your life to be unexplainable apart from God? (Answer *not at all, somewhat,* or *to a great degree.*) What do you find appealing or unappealing about experiencing the "unexplainable"?

3. Can you think of any ways in which you as a person or the unfolding events of your life to date are unexplainable apart from God?

4. Have you ever made a decision that appeared to make little or no sense to others, but clearly reflected God's leading in your life? Explain what occurred and how you were motivated to follow through with such a decision.

5. Has God ever done something in or through your life for which the only logical explanation is "God did it"? If so, describe this experience. Also describe anything like this that may have occurred recently in the life of someone you know.

6. How did the experiences you just described in response to the previous question enable you or someone you know to point to God?

7. What would you like to see God do in you personally that would qualify as "unexplainable apart from God"? (Some examples: Helping you overcome a bad habit, or be able to truly forgive someone who has wronged you, or to change your attitude concerning something or someone, or to change something else about you.)

8. In what current circumstance or situation do you need God to do
   something that only He can do? (Examples: Healing a relationship that seems broken beyond repair, meeting a financial need,
   bringing physical healing, or bringing some sort of resolution to a
   current conflict or trial.)

PART ONE

UNEXPLAINABLE CONTENTMENT

Lifeshift 1: From Outside-In to Inside-Out

2

SO DESIRED, YET SO ELUSIVE

I have learned to be content in whatever circumstances I am.

PHILIPPIANS 4:11

Few things in life are so elusive as contentment.

This discovery dates all the way back to Adam and Eve, who had everything anyone could ever want or need—except for the fruit from that one particular tree. *If only we could taste that fruit,* they thought.

Ever since, mankind has been plagued with a severe case of the if-only's. We all think, *I'd be content if only I had ... if only I were ... if only I weren't ... if only I looked like ... if only I hadn't ... if only they hadn't ... if only things were ... if only I owned ... if only I could ...*

For most of us, contentment always seems to be one or two if-only's away. This is why I find the apostle Paul's words in Philippians 4:11–12 so amazing:

> Not that I speak from want, for I have learned to be content in whatever circumstances I am. I know how to get

along with humble means, and I also know how to live in
prosperity; in any and every circumstance I have learned
the secret of being filled and going hungry, both of having
abundance and suffering need.

Paul had discovered the cure for the if-only's. He'd learned the *secret* of
being content in spite of undesirable circumstances.

If such contentment is truly attainable—then *I want it.* Don't you?

Oh, to be truly content! The dictionary defines contentment as "freedom from dissatisfaction, anxiety, or agitation,"[1] or "wanting no more than
one has," or being "satisfied with things as they are." It's not complacency,
but something much more profound and satisfying. I think of contentment
as soul-satisfaction, being at peace, at rest within, in need of nothing more
or different. Who doesn't want that?

So why is such contentment so elusive? Why does our experience so
often reflect the very opposite: unrest, agitation, frustration, dissatisfaction,
longing, searching, and striving?

What It Takes (Outwardly)

Let me offer for your consideration a simple truth about me and perhaps
you: My experience of contentment is determined almost completely by
the outward conditions and circumstances of life. This is the exact opposite
of what Paul is describing. For me, when life's good (going as I want it
to go), I'm content; when life's not so good (not going as I'd like it to),
contentment fades or is lost altogether.

I can easily form my list of conditions and circumstances that bring me
contentment:

- Mary Ann and I are enjoying our marriage relationship.
- All three of our kids are healthy and thriving in their
  respective ventures.

- My extended family members and friends are healthy and basically happy.
- My work-related efforts are being met with success.
- My health and the health of those around me is good.
- There's enough money in the bank to meet all our needs and at least some of our wants.
- My friendships are enjoyable, meaningful, and at peace.
- Nothing significant is broken around the house, and the cars are running smoothly.
- I have some "things" that help make life enjoyable.
- My favorite sports teams are winning.
- The weather's good. (Sunny and 75° to 85° is ideal.)
- The writing of this book is flowing freely.
- I sense that God and I are operating on the same page, and He's smiling upon me.

As you can see, it doesn't take much to make me feel content(!).

Perhaps you too have a list—maybe a bit shorter, maybe longer. Of course, contentment comes in varying degrees, as some things on our lists are significantly higher in value than others. But you get the idea.

How often do I live with a high level of contentment? Based on my list above—I think I can recall one Thursday about four years ago … that was a good day.

All kidding aside, just how often are the conditions and circumstances of life just as we want them to be? And in those rare, rare times when they are, how long do they remain that way?

Outside-In

With our contentment so closely linked to our outward conditions and circumstances, it's easy to understand why it's so elusive. The truth is, conditions and circumstances are seldom the way we want them to be. That's why so many of us are agitated, frustrated, dissatisfied, angry—and driving and striving for something more, something different. Most of us are suffering from a severe case of the if-only's.

We need to understand that true contentment is an "inside job" that will never be attained in any lasting way by "outside" factors. We work so hard to shape and control those outward conditions and circumstances of life, believing we'll then achieve contentment on the inside. I call this the "outside-in" approach to life.

There's only one problem with this approach: It doesn't work. This is why I find Paul's words so amazing. He's speaking of an "inside-out" approach to life. He has found a way to shape and control his "inside," such that what goes on "outside" has no effect on his level of contentment. Read once again what he states:

> Not that I speak from want, for I have learned to be content in whatever circumstances I am. I know how to get along with humble means, and I also know how to live in prosperity; in any and every circumstance I have learned the secret of being filled and going hungry, both of having abundance and suffering need. (Phil. 4:11–12)

He's claiming there's a way to be content even when …
- There isn't enough money in the bank to pay the bills.
- We can't buy what we really want.
- One of our kids is struggling.
- Married life becomes hard work.
- A friend causes hurt.
- The big sale falls through.
- The doctor says, "Yes, it's cancer."
- The boss says, "We're downsizing."

- Twelve inches of snow falls overnight, and the snowblower won't start.
- Our favorite teams keep losing.
- Our investments are shrinking in value.
- The dentist says, "You need a root canal."
- You've failed to do what you set out to do.
- Someone you were depending on failed to do what they said they would do.
- You're sick and can't afford to be sick.
- You're stuck in bumper-to-bumper traffic.
- You receive the news that a loved one has died.

Even in times like that, Paul says, *I've learned to be content in whatever circumstances I am.*

Wow!

More Than Happiness

It's important here to point out that I'm not equating contentment with happiness. Happiness is defined as "having, showing or marked by feelings of joy or pleasure," but I don't believe Paul is saying, "I'm feeling happy about being hungry, and cold, and suffering need." Rather he's saying that in spite of those things, "I'm content, at peace within; I'm genuinely okay with where I am in these difficult circumstances, and I'm free from dissatisfaction, anxiety, and agitation."

Happiness is only a feeling, and while Paul is certainly talking about something that touches upon feelings, it's much deeper and far more meaningful. Happiness isn't the goal; contentment is.

Although the outside-in approach to gaining contentment is the norm, it doesn't work. This explains why most of us are working so hard to maneuver the conditions and circumstances of our lives into the way we want them to be. We drive ourselves to fulfill all of our if-only's, believing that doing so will make us content. But even the few who are sometimes able to fulfill their if-only's soon discover that their contentment quickly disappears as conditions or circumstances change.

Outside-in is not God's way to contentment, for God wants us to experience lasting contentment. He wants each of us to possess the contentment of which Paul writes—contentment that's unexplainable apart from God. This is exactly what Paul refers to a few verses earlier: "And the peace of God, *which surpasses all comprehension,* will guard your hearts and your minds in Christ Jesus" (Phil. 4:7).

Jesus speaks of it as well:

> Peace I leave with you; My peace I give to you; not as the world gives do I give to you. Do not let your heart be troubled, nor let it be fearful. (John 14:27)

Here's a peace, a contentment, that's not dependent upon outward factors. It's the same peace Paul discovered, and it comes from God, who works from the inside out.

God Always Starts on the Inside

Perhaps you recall the account in the Bible of when God sent His prophet Samuel to a man named Jesse, in order to choose a new king from among Jesse's sons (1 Sam. 16:1–13). Jesse had eight sons, seven of whom he brought to the "king draft" that day in response to Samuel's request.

As those seven eldest sons of Jesse assembled before him, Samuel "looked at Eliab and thought, 'Surely the LORD's anointed is before Him'" (16:6). By sheer physical appearance, Jesse's oldest son, Eliab, looked like the total package. In Samuel's eyes, he had "king" written all over him. But not in God's eyes:

> But the LORD said to Samuel, "Do not look at his appear-
> ance or at the height of his stature, because I have rejected
> him; for God sees not as man sees, for man looks at the out-
> ward appearance, but the LORD looks at the heart." (16:7)

One by one, seven of Jesse's sons were presented before Samuel—and all seven were passed over by the Lord.

At this point, Samuel was no doubt perplexed, since God had clearly stated He would choose a king from among Jesse's sons.

> And Samuel said to Jesse, "Are these all the children?"

> And he said, "There remains yet the youngest, and behold,
> he is tending the sheep."

> Then Samuel said to Jesse, "Send and bring him; for we
> will not sit down until he comes here." (16:11)

This youngest son, the shepherd boy, was so much the unexplainable choice that he hadn't even been invited. As it turned out, young David *was* the choice—because he possessed the *heart* God was looking for.

God always begins on the inside. He always starts with the heart. This is where He does His greatest work, for this is what ultimately matters.

If you want to discover the contentment of which Paul speaks, you'll need to make what I'm calling a *lifeshift* from an *outside-in* approach to life to an *inside-out* approach. To make this lifeshift, we need to discover the same "secret" that Paul says he learned. Over the next five chapters, I want to spell out five secrets Paul reveals in Philippians 4 which enabled him to experi- ence "the peace of God, which surpasses all comprehension"—a contentment that's unattainable and unexplainable apart from God.

Discussion Questions

1. To what degree do you suffer from a case of the "if-only's"? (Use a one-to-ten scale: 1 = *not at all*; 10 = *severely*.) Explain your answer.
2. How would you explain the difference between being *content* and being *complacent*?
3. What outward conditions and circumstances have the biggest effect on your level of contentment?
4. Can you recall a time when you experienced the "peace of God, which surpasses all comprehension"?

3

CONTENTMENT'S FIRST SECRET

Rejoice in the Lord

Rejoice in the Lord always; again I will say, rejoice!

PHILIPPIANS 4:4

Perhaps no setting provides us with a more visible demonstration of rejoicing than the world of sports.

You've probably watched the players on a baseball team charge the pitcher's mound and pile on one another in sheer jubilation after recording the final out to win a championship. Or you've seen football players dance, chest-bump, or pat one another on the backside after scoring a touchdown. If tennis is your game, you've seen champions toss their racket in the air and fall to their knees in utter relief. NASCAR drivers seem to enjoy doing doughnuts on the infield and backflips as they exit their car. Olympic champions, draped in their country's flag, run victory laps.

I remember watching Michael Jordan hug and kiss the championship trophy following the Bulls' first NBA championship. Kissing the trophy has now become common practice. Professional hockey players skate around the rink carrying Lord Stanley's Cup high overhead. Even golfers, ladies and gentlemen that they are, find expression for rejoicing by fist-pumping and hugging their caddie after holing the winning putt.

Winning is reason for rejoicing. And I can say with certainty, there'll never be greater reason for rejoicing than when my Chicago Cubs finally win the World Series.

What causes you to rejoice? While most of us will never experience the above, we do find reason to rejoice—getting accepted by the college we wanted most to attend, getting a date with that person we thought was out of our league, marrying that person, experiencing the birth of a child, buying a new house or car, seeing our child make the team or the honor roll, completing the big sale or project at work, receiving a promotion, receiving a year-end bonus. We rejoice when vacation begins, or the doctor gives a clean bill of health, or our favorite team wins, or we break eighty for the first time on the golf course.

There are many, many reasons to rejoice. And this is good. Life is hard and filled with challenges, and when something occurs over which we can rejoice, by all means rejoice. In fact, we would benefit from taking more time to rejoice when there's a good reason.

Beware

We need to recognize, however, that such rejoicing depends upon outward conditions and circumstances. Therefore, there are some truths we need to be aware of:

1. *Rejoicing that depends on outward conditions and circumstances is* not *guaranteed.* It's never a sure bet, a certainty you can count on. You may never get the promotion or the year-end bonus. Your child may not make the team or the honor roll. The big sale may not go through. Your team may never win the championship (as a lifelong Cubs fan, I know). You may never be able to afford a new house or car. Your dream date may have dreams that don't include you. A clean bill of health isn't guaranteed every year.

If your rejoicing depends on outward conditions and circumstances, there's no guarantee you'll rejoice.

2. *Rejoicing that depends on outward conditions and circumstances can be taken away.* The dream job you celebrated a year ago is gone due to a downsizing. The retirement funds you were counting on are dramatically reduced when the stock market drops. The cancer that was in remission now returns. The person you thought was "the one" now says, "Let's just be friends." The very conditions and circumstances that caused rejoicing can be reversed, and your rejoicing taken away.

3. *Rejoicing that depends on outward conditions and circumstances is temporary.* The smell of a new car is gone in a matter of months. The celebration that followed the completion of the big sale is now followed by the challenge of completing the next sale. Vacation is over, and it's time to go back to work or school. The trophy that once produced feelings of euphoria now only produces fond memories.

4. *The outward conditions and circumstances that potentially bring rejoicing can also bring heartache.* Your child doesn't make the team. The sale falls through. A friend or loved one dies suddenly. The job you really wanted is given to someone else. An unexpected expense wipes out the vacation budget. The pregnancy turns into a miscarriage. You receive a letter of rejection.

When our reason to rejoice is taken away or fades away, or turns to heartache, our level of contentment usually follows suit.

The Roller Coaster

I recall a Saturday this past spring when I, as a father, had specific reason to rejoice. Our son Kyle pitched his team to victory in a big baseball game. Our other son, Kirk, quarterbacked his team to victory in the spring football game, and our daughter, Karalyne, and her partner won a big tennis match. As a result, all three kids, along with mom and dad, were rejoicing.

I drove home that evening not only rejoicing, but content. It had been a good day.

But I also recall the day Kyle's baseball team lost the district championship to a team they'd already beaten twice in the regular season. Or the day we returned from the doctor's office after being told that Kirk's ankle was broken and his football season, only one game old, was over. Or the day Karalyne and her partner lost the doubles championship in straight sets. On those occasions, to the degree that victory provides a reason for rejoicing, I wasn't rejoicing; nor was I very content.

There's a relationship between rejoicing and contentment. To know one is to know the other; to be denied one is to be denied the other. If our ability to rejoice depends upon outward conditions and circumstances, then our experience with contentment will come and go as conditions and circumstances change.

This explains why so many people live life on an emotional roller coaster—one day up, the next day down. As their rejoicing goes, so goes their contentment.

Contentment's First Secret

Paul understood the relationship between rejoicing and contentment. And he learned a secret about rejoicing that enabled him to be content even when things were "down." He reveals this secret in Philippians 4:4: "Rejoice in the Lord always; again I will say, rejoice!"

We need to learn as Paul did to rejoice in that which is guaranteed—a sure thing, a certainty, something (or someone) we can always count on. We need to learn to rejoice in that which cannot be taken away—ever. We need to learn to rejoice in that which produces lasting satisfaction, and that not only doesn't fade, but gets even better and stronger over time. And we need to learn to rejoice over that which gives us the strength and ability to face heartache.

That's why Paul tells us to rejoice in the Lord. The Lord is someone we can always count on; He's a sure thing, a guarantee. He cannot be taken away; He's always present. The Lord not only offers lasting satisfaction, but ever-increasing satisfaction. As David said, "O taste and see that the LORD is good" (Ps. 34:8). He produces hope and strength to face heartache. And because the Lord is within us, His presence and participation in our lives isn't dependent on outward conditions and circumstances.

Therefore, if we learn as Paul did to rejoice in the Lord, then in spite of what's going on around us we can experience contentment—contentment that is unattainable and unexplainable apart from God.

Five Ways to Rejoice in the Lord

So what does it mean to *rejoice in the Lord?*

Let me try and explain by giving you five ways to rejoice in the Lord.

1. Rejoice over who He is.

If you want to get a good sampling of what it means to rejoice over who He is, read the Psalms.

Take Psalm 103, for example. David begins, "Bless the LORD, O my soul, and all that is within me, bless His holy name." David stops to consider who the Lord is, and from his soul—from "all that is within" him—comes rejoicing.

In the verses that follow, David considers how the Lord is the One who pardons sins, who ultimately heals all our diseases, who redeems us, and who crowns us with lovingkindness and compassion. He's the One who satisfies our years with good things and renews our strength each and every day. All His deeds are righteous, and His judgments are for the oppressed. "The LORD is compassionate and gracious, slow to anger and abounding in lovingkindness" (103:8).

Thankfully, God hasn't dealt with us according to our sins against Him, as David reminds us. As high as the heavens are above the earth, so is His love for those who call Him Lord. He has taken our sins from us and tossed them to the opposite end of the universe. As a father has compassion on his children, so does He on His children. And He knows us inside out. He knows just how fragile we are, and the lovingkindness He displays to us is never-ending.

He sits on the throne of the universe and holds all things in the palm of His hand. All of His creation rejoices in who He is.

Throughout twenty-two verses, David rejoices in all these facets of who God is. Then one last time David says, "Bless the LORD, O my soul!"

All that in just one psalm!

So take stock of who God is, and you'll find yourself rejoicing, like David, with all that is within you.

2. Rejoice over what He has done for you.

Perhaps the most famous verse in all the Bible says it best: "For God so loved the world, that He gave His only begotten Son, that whoever believes in Him shall not perish, but have eternal life" (John 3:16).

What has God done? He gave the life of His Son in exchange for you and me. The Son willingly laid down His life so you and I could have eternal life. Jesus bore the full expression of God's wrath against sin so that we wouldn't have to.

If you've seen the movie *The Passion of the Christ,* you have a pretty good picture of what Jesus endured for you. This is reason for great rejoicing: Your sins can be forgiven—completely. Your guilt can be wiped away—totally. You're offered freedom from the power of sin, and the chance to become a member of God's family for all eternity, all because of what He has done for you.

This is cause for rejoicing every day, in spite of life's difficult conditions and circumstances.

3. Rejoice over His thoughts and feelings about you.

Listen to the words of Jesus in Luke's gospel about the extent of God's care and concern for you:

> Are not five sparrows sold for two cents? Yet not one of them is forgotten before God. Indeed, *the very hairs of your head are all numbered.* Do not fear; you are more valuable than many sparrows. (Luke 12:6–7)

A few chapters later in Luke, we hear Jesus telling three different parables—of a lost sheep, a lost coin, and a lost son—all in an attempt to make clear just how God and all of heaven feel about every lost soul. As a punch line at the end of the first parable, Jesus says, "I tell you that in the same way, there will be more joy in heaven over one sinner who repents than over ninety-nine righteous persons who need no repentance" (Luke 15:7).

As a punch line at the end of the second parable, Jesus says, "In the same way, I tell you, there is joy in the presence of the angels of God over one sinner who repents" (15:10).

And at the end of the third parable, a father throws the party of all parties because of the return of his prodigal son: "For this son of mine was dead and has come to life again; he was lost and has been found" (15:24).

In these parables Jesus is asking us, "Do you have any idea how strongly My Father in heaven feels about you?"

This is reason for rejoicing. No matter what's going on in your life today, you're loved and cared for by your heavenly Father. God Himself says to you,

> Do not fear, for I have redeemed you; I have called you by name; you are Mine! When you pass through the waters, I will be with you; and through the rivers, they will not overflow you. When you walk through the fire, you will not be scorched, nor will the flame burn you. For I am the LORD your God, the Holy One of Israel, your Savior. (Isa. 43:1–3)

What better reason to rejoice!

4. Rejoice over His desire to participate in your life.

God's care for us is not from a distance. His care is intimate; He places His Spirit within us. When Jesus told His disciples that it was to their advantage that He go away (John 16:7), it must have sounded like the most off-the-wall statement these men had ever heard. But He went on to explain: "For if I do not go away, the Helper [The Holy Spirit] will not come to you."

A few verses later Jesus explains the impact of the Holy Spirit:

> But when He, the Spirit of truth, comes, He will guide you into all the truth; for He will not speak on His own initiative, but whatever He hears, He will speak; and He will disclose to you what is to come. (16:13)

Because God wants to participate in your life every moment of every day, He places His presence within you in the form of His Holy Spirit.

It's this great fact that caused Paul to ask rhetorically, "If God is for us, who is against us?" and, "Who will separate us from the love of Christ?" (Rom. 8:31, 35). Regardless of what may be going on around us, if we have God within, there's reason to rejoice.

5. Rejoice over His promises to you.

The Bible contains hundreds of God's promises given to those who know Him. Here are just a few:

> Blessed is the man who trusts in the LORD and whose trust is the LORD. (Jer. 17:7)

> The LORD is near to the brokenhearted and saves those who are crushed in spirit. (Ps. 34:18)

> This is the confidence which we have before Him, that, if we ask anything according to His will, He hears us. (1 John 5:14)

> Be strong and courageous, do not be afraid or tremble at them, for the LORD your God is the one who goes with you. He will not fail you or forsake you. (Deut. 31:6)

> Call to Me and I will answer you, and I will tell you great and mighty things, which you do not know. (Jer. 33:3)

> Trust in the LORD with all your heart and do not lean on your own understanding. In all your ways acknowledge Him, and He will make your paths straight. (Prov. 3:5–6)

"For I know the plans that I have for you," declares the LORD, "plans for welfare and not for calamity to give you a future and a hope." (Jer. 29:11)

Cast your burden upon the LORD and He will sustain you; He will never allow the righteous to be shaken. (Ps. 55:22)

But the Lord is faithful, and He will strengthen and protect you from the evil one. (2 Thess. 3:3)

And my God will supply all your needs according to His riches in glory in Christ Jesus. (Phil. 4:19)

And we know that God causes all things to work together for good to those who love God, to those who are called according to His purpose. (Rom. 8:28)

Yet those who wait for the LORD will gain new strength; they will mount up with wings like eagles, they will run and not get tired, they will walk and not become weary. (Isa. 40:31)

For the eyes of the LORD are toward the righteous, and His ears attend to their prayer, but the face of the LORD is against those who do evil. (1 Peter 3:12)

These promises are the source of true rejoicing, for they're guaranteed—they're for today, tomorrow, and every day to come. Nothing and no one can take them away. And never do they mean more than when life's conditions and circumstances bring heartache.

This is why Paul says, "Rejoice in the Lord always; again I will say, rejoice!"

- Consider who God is.
- Reflect on what He has done for you.
- Take stock of His thoughts and feelings about you.
- Grab hold of His desire to participate in your life.
- And claim His promises for you.

All these provide true reason to rejoice, giving us the basis for contentment in spite of life's circumstances—the contentment that's unexplainable apart from God.

Discussion Questions

1. In what ways do your reasons for rejoicing impact your level of contentment? Be specific.
2. What "outside" conditions and circumstances are giving you reason to rejoice currently?
3. What "outside" conditions and circumstances are making it difficult for you to rejoice currently?
4. This chapter lists ways to "rejoice in the Lord." In what ways can you personally apply these suggestions? Be specific and practical.

4

CONTENTMENT'S SECOND SECRET

Pray about Everything

Be anxious for nothing, but in everything by
prayer and supplication with thanksgiving let
your requests be made known to God.

PHILIPPIANS 4:6

In his famous "Song of the Year" Grammy Award-winner in the late '80s, Bobby McFerrin told everyone, "Don't Worry, Be Happy!"

Don't you wish it were that easy?

Unfortunately, it's not. Just telling yourself not to worry won't make worry go away. There's no switch to simply turn it off.

Worry accompanies life. It's a fact of our existence.

And what do we worry about?

Just about everything. We worry about money or the lack thereof. Those who have it worry about investing it wisely so they'll always have it. Those who don't have it worry about the implications.

We worry about people and relationships.

Parents worry about children, and eventually children about parents.

We enter a new arena—be it work, school, or neighborhood—and we worry about being liked and accepted.

We worry about our job: *Will I be able to cut it? Will my company be able to cut it?*

We worry about the future and the future of those we love.

As we grow older, we worry about our health and the health of those we love.

We worry about getting everything on our to-do list accomplished.

We worry about little things like getting to our flight on time, and big things like *Is my cancer treatable?* Those big things are the biggest source of worry. I call them Goliaths. They're those conditions and circumstances over which we have little or no control, those matters that far exceed the resources we possess to address them. Life is filled with Goliaths. Hence we worry.

Polar Opposites

We all have a worry list, little things and big things. And to the degree that we keep going over our list, we forfeit contentment.

Worry and contentment are polar opposites, and mutually exclusive. When one is present, the other's absent. Worry is a contentment stealer. It robs us of the contentment we so long to possess.

So if we're to experience contentment, we must face and defeat worry. The question is … how?

There are two options for overcoming worry:

Option 1: Control your outward conditions and circumstances.

All of us, to one degree or another, are working with this option. We're all trying to manipulate the conditions and circumstances of life to get free from worry. We believe that if we can just get everything and everyone in our life to be as we want them to be, we'll have nothing to worry about.

There's only one problem: It can't be done. No matter how vast our personal resources, or how much control we hold, there'll always be factors outside of our control. Just ask those who lost loved ones on 9/11, or those who lost their homes on the Gulf Coast when Katrina blew through, or anyone who has ever heard their doctor say, "It's cancer, and it's not treatable."

Try as we may to control our outside conditions and circumstances in order to overcome worry, we can't do it. That's why the outside-in approach to contentment doesn't work.

Option 2: Give everything over to God's control.

Worry is an internal condition, an "inside job," if you will, and therefore must be addressed from within. This explains why Paul writes what he does in Philippians 4:6–7:

> Be anxious for nothing, but *in everything by prayer and supplication with thanksgiving let your requests be made known to God.* And the peace of God, which surpasses all comprehension, will guard your hearts and your minds in Christ Jesus.

This is the second secret: *Pray about everything.* Exchange worry for prayer.

This is what Paul says he has learned to do. Instead of worrying about the matters on your list, bring your list—all of it—before God in prayer.

Note Paul's choice of words: "Be anxious for *nothing*, but in *everything* by prayer …" Paul's an extremist! What should we be anxious (worried) about? *Nothing!* And what should we bring before God in prayer? *Everything!*

Paul himself has learned to do this, and he has needed to. A few verses earlier he noted a conflict brewing in the Philippian church between two people (4:2), and it was creating a problem. Paul was concerned enough about this conflict that he addressed it in this letter to the church.

Even bigger on his own worry list was the matter of his own future. As he wrote, he sat in prison, chained to two soldiers while awaiting a trial to determine whether he would live or die.

So Paul had reason to worry. Yet he *wasn't* worried; he had learned to be content in any and all circumstances. He had discovered a secret: *Pray about everything.*

By Prayer and Supplication

What does such prayer include?

Paul tells us: "In everything *by prayer and supplication with thanksgiving* let your requests be made known to God." So significant is the phrase "with thanksgiving" that I'm going to treat it separately in the next chapter. For now, let's focus on the significance of those words *prayer* and *supplication.*

The "and" between these two words is significant. It implies that they carry different meanings. Supplication is defined as "making a humble and earnest request; asking humbly and earnestly." Prayer is typically defined as making requests to God. Yet Paul makes a distinction between making requests (supplication) and prayer.

So what does Paul mean by "prayer"?

Going back to when Jesus' disciples asked Him to teach them to pray, we find this answer from Him:

Pray, then, in this way: "Our Father who is in heaven, hallowed be Your name.

"Your kingdom come. Your will be done, on earth as it is in heaven.

"Give us this day our daily bread.

"And forgive us our debts, as we also have forgiven our debtors.

"And do not lead us into temptation, but deliver us from evil. [For Yours is the kingdom and the power and the glory forever. Amen.]" (Matt. 6:9–13)

It's important to note here that Jesus didn't begin with requests. Instead He began with worship. Prayer begins with *taking stock of who God is*: "Our Father who is in heaven, hallowed be Your name" (6:9). Jesus' disciples were to begin by addressing their heavenly Dad. The word Jesus used that has been translated "Father" could also be translated as "Daddy." While both words can clearly refer to the same person, there's an intimacy and warmth captured by that word *Daddy*. This is the one to whom we bring everything.

And how good and important is it to know that He's holy—perfect (His name is *hallowed*). This means His love for us is perfect, His wisdom concerning the affairs of our life is perfect, His goodness displayed toward us is perfect, and His power in using His limitless resources on our behalf is perfect.

No wonder Paul wants us to take stock of who God is!

Worship was to be followed by confession, which is a normal response to the acknowledgment of God's holiness. In this way, we're taking stock not only of who God is, but also of who we are by comparison. Before we ever utter one word in the way of request, we need to comprehend who God is and who we are before Him. Such understanding puts all our requests in perspective. This is the perspective we so desperately need before making requests of God.

Confession is then followed by submission. "Your kingdom come. Your will be done, on earth as it is in heaven." Prayer includes the surrender of my will to God's will, and the submission of self to God. Before uttering one word in the way of supplication, prayer has taken us to the worship of God, confession before God, and submission to God. Having this under-standing of prayer will certainly shape our attitude in every request we bring before God.

He's Near

I recall as a young boy how safe I felt when I was around my dad. I remem-ber one particular trip to summer camp with the Boy Scout troop he led as Scoutmaster. I was really young, perhaps five or six years old. We left home on a Friday evening for Camp Owassippe, a few hours away. We were scheduled to arrive late that night, well after dark.

While it happened too many years ago for me to remember all the details, I do vividly remember coming to a dead end in the road once we reached the camp; obviously we weren't where we were supposed to be. And boy, was it dark! Apart from the headlights on the car, you couldn't see the hand in front of your face.

I recall sitting in the front seat next to my dad, thinking, *No problem, my dad's here. Dad will figure it out, he always does.* As a young boy, I had no reason to worry if dad was present. Had he not been there, I would have felt very differently. In the same way, Paul is telling us, "The Lord is near—there's nothing to be worried about!"

Taking stock of who our heavenly Dad is can do a lot to cure even the most serious case of the worries. Consider Psalm 46, which begins,

God is our refuge and strength, a very present help in trouble. Therefore we will not fear, though the earth should change and though the mountains slip into the heart of the sea.

And ends this way:

"Cease striving and know that I am God; I will be exalted among the nations, I will be exalted in the earth." The LORD of hosts is with us; the God of Jacob is our stronghold.

Such prayer also has a way of removing self-centered and self-focused supplication. I think of the words of James: "You ask and do not receive, because you ask with wrong motives, so that you may spend it on your pleasures" (James 4:3). The heart and mind that have been caught up in worship of the living God, in confession of sin in light of God's holiness, and in surrender of one's will to God will be ready and rightly motivated for supplication. This, I believe, is what Paul meant when he mentions *both* "prayer and supplication" in Philippians 4.

Ready to Make Requests

Paul goes on to mention supplication and bringing our requests humbly before God. The apostle Peter expressed the same thing this way:

Therefore humble yourselves under the mighty hand of God, that He may exalt you at the proper time, casting all your anxiety [worries] on Him, because He cares for you. (1 Peter 5:6–7)

Peter, too, is an extremist; he says we're to cast *all* our anxiety on the Lord. We're to take our worry list—both little things and big ones—and bring them and ourselves before God in humble surrender.

As we do that, let's be clear about one thing: Making our requests known to God is more for our benefit than His. After all, He knows all things. As Jesus reminded us, "Your Father knows what you need before you ask Him" (Matt. 6:8). Bringing our list before God is for the purpose of offloading our list onto His broad shoulders, thereby inviting Him to intervene according to His will.

And what's the result of doing so?

Paul answers: "The peace of God, which surpasses all comprehension, will guard your hearts and your minds in Christ Jesus."

When we take our list before God and humbly turn it over to His capable care, we receive in return His peace and contentment. It's a peace, Paul says, that "surpasses all comprehension"—it's unexplainable apart from God. You can't explain how you can know such contentment in the midst of adverse conditions and circumstances, but you do. You can't really articulate how it comes or why you feel as calm as you do. It surpasses comprehension; it seems inconceivable; it's indescribable and unexplainable.

This is exactly what Paul is experiencing as he's writing while being chained to two soldiers, awaiting a trial that will determine whether he lives or dies. How can he be content at such a time? It's the peace of God that surpasses all comprehension.

Both Thoughts and Feelings

This peace, this contentment, covers both thoughts and feelings. It will "guard your *hearts and your minds* in Christ Jesus," Paul says. We experience a great confidence (in our thoughts) and a great soul-rest (in our feelings). This peace replaces worry, in spite of outside conditions and circumstances. This is the result of "prayer and supplication."

So why do so many of us still battle worry on a daily basis?

The answer may simply be that we fail to take the necessary time to bring ourselves and our "list" before God. Instead, we're hard at work pursuing that first option—trying to control outward conditions and circumstances in the false assumption that we can, in fact, succeed in exercising that control to eliminate worry.

But God says, "Cease striving and know that I am God" (Ps. 46:10). Thirty *less* minutes of striving each day and thirty *more* minutes devoted to prayer and supplication will be well worth the exchange.

Why not give it a try? Try it for a week or a month—and see if you're not able to say, "Whatever circumstances I'm in, I've learned to be content."

Discussion Questions

1. What are you tempted to worry about today? (Identify your top three.)

2. What impact do those worries have on your level of content-ment? How are you affected physically, mentally, emotionally, spiritually, and relationally?

3. How would you explain the difference between *prayer* and *supplication*?

4. What percentage of your communication with God is made up of prayer (worship, confession, and submission) and what percentage is made up of supplication (requests)?

5. What will you take away from these three chapters (2, 3, and 4) and this discussion of them? Be as specific and practical as possible.

5

CONTENTMENT'S THIRD SECRET

Celebrate Thanksgiving Every Day

*Be anxious for nothing, but in everything by
prayer and supplication with thanksgiving let
your requests be made known to God.*

PHILIPPIANS 4:6

Thanksgiving is definitely one of my favorite holidays, especially considering the five "*f*'s" it includes: faith, family, food, football, and a four-day weekend. As far as I'm concerned, that's a tough combination to beat.

And talk about positive and upbeat! Pausing to express gratitude for one's blessings breathes life into anyone's soul. Even in times of trial and heartache, when it's most difficult to see life's glass as half full instead of half empty, stopping to give thanks makes a difference.

Thanksgiving's such a great holiday—it's a shame we celebrate it only once a year. Maybe we should change that fact.

Consider again Paul's words in Philippines 4:6: "Be anxious for nothing, but in everything by prayer and supplication *with thanksgiving* let your requests be made known to God." I see that phrase "with thanksgiving" as the third secret that Paul learned, enabling him to find contentment in spite of his circumstances. Thanksgiving is indeed a critical ingredient.

A Partnership

Paul's wording here is important to note. There's a partnership here; prayer and supplication are not to be engaged in alone, but rather "with thanksgiving."

When you take stock of who God is—wise, powerful, good, loving, gracious, merciful, and so much more—give thanks for those qualities.

When you recognize that absolutely nothing can happen to you apart from God's knowledge of us and His love for us, give thanks.

When you consider all that He has done for you, starting with the giving of His one and only Son, give thanks.

As you reflect upon His desire to be intimately acquainted with all of the affairs of your life, give thanks.

As you contemplate just how precious you are to Him, give thanks.

To know that the One who holds the universe in the palm of His hand also holds you there—this, too, is reason to continually give thanks.

And when you find yourself clinging to one of His promises, give thanks for both the promise and its guaranteed fulfillment.

All this is what Paul means when he writes, "by prayer ... *with thanksgiving.*"

And it doesn't stop there. When we humbly bring ourselves and our requests before God (in supplication), we should do that "with thanksgiving." What a privilege to be able to bring our requests before Him, and what a benefit to know that He'll answer in a way and in a time that are perfect for us. These truths provide us with good reason to give thanks.

Cause for Celebration

This partnership between prayer and thanksgiving is very important both to God and to us. Let me offer four reasons why it's so crucial that we learn this third secret of celebrating Thanksgiving every day.

1. Giving thanks reminds us of God's past provision and protection.

And boy, do we need the reminder! How quickly we forget; how easily we lose sight. This is and has always been the way of human nature. It's why God instructed His people during Old Testament times to establish certain holidays and celebrate them annually. He didn't want His people to forget His promises to provide and protect.

Consider, for example, what happened on the night of the original Passover:

> For I will go through the land of Egypt on that night, and will strike down all the firstborn in the land of Egypt, both man and beast; and against all the gods of Egypt I will execute judgments—I am the LORD. The blood shall be a sign for you on the houses where you live; and when I see the blood I will pass over you, and no plague will befall you to destroy you when I strike the land of Egypt. (Ex. 12:12–13)

Moses instructed the people of Israel to take the blood of a lamb and spread it over the doorposts of their house so that when the angel of death passed over that night, he would see the blood of the lamb and spare them. The tenth and final plague against Egypt—the slaying of the firstborn sons—thus opened the door for the Israelites to leave Egypt after four hundred years of captivity. It was obviously a significant event that God didn't want His people to forget. Therefore He instructed that the Passover be celebrated every year for generations to come:

> And you shall observe this event as an ordinance for you
> and your children forever. When you enter the land which
> the LORD will give you, as He has promised, you shall
> observe this rite. (12:24–25)

God wanted His people to be reminded at least once a year, in a very tangible way, of His provision and protection. The Passover was a time of giving thanks for who God is, for what He had done, and for what He promised to do in the future.

This same principle is put forth in the New Testament through the celebration of the Lord's Supper. We're instructed and encouraged to observe the Lord's Supper so we never forget all that Jesus' death and resurrection accomplished for us.

This giving of thanks for Christ and the cross is especially important when the conditions and circumstances of life tempt us to think and feel that God has forgotten us, or He's unaware, or He's simply preoccupied. We need to stop and give thanks so that we're reminded of who God is, what He has done for us, and what He promises to do in the future. We cannot afford to forget or lose sight of God's provision and protection.

I keep a prayer journal and have done so for years. My journal is broken down into three sections, with the third devoted to recording the evidences of God's presence in, around, and through my life. I learned long ago that if I don't take time to reflect on His participation in my life and make the effort to record it, then I forget. I lose sight so quickly, so easily, of what God has done on my behalf.

I find this section of my journal to be especially important when times get tough and I inevitably begin wondering why He isn't intervening to make them easier. As I reread my entries from previous days, weeks, and months, I'm reminded of God's provision and protection and naturally find myself giving thanks. Furthermore, I'm encouraged in heart and strengthened in faith.

Whatever it takes, we need to celebrate thanksgiving every day to remind ourselves of God's commitment to provide and protect.

2. Giving thanks is an expression of faith.

When we include thanksgiving as we lay our requests before God, we're in effect saying to God, "I believe that You're hearing this request and will respond in a way that's best for me, at just the right time." We're giving thanks, in advance, for what we believe He's going to do.

This is a clear expression of faith. The writer of Hebrews says, "Now faith is the assurance of things hoped for, the conviction of things not seen" (Heb. 11:1). When we give thanks in advance, we're expressing confidence in God's ability to provide and protect in the future.

Why's that important? It has to do with how God feels about faith. The writer of Hebrews continues, "And *without faith it is impossible to please Him,* for he who comes to God must believe that He is and that He is a rewarder of those who seek Him" (11:6). God is absolutely thrilled when we demonstrate faith in Him. To pray and humbly make requests *with thanksgiving* displays a faith that God longs to see from His children.

When my boys were very young, they loved to climb on the top bunk of their beds and jump into my arms. Kyle, the oldest, jumped without hesitation, having full confidence I would catch him. Kirk, on the other hand, wasn't so sure. Perhaps because he was two years younger, he always insisted on holding my hand before jumping.

Then one night I told Kirk before he jumped that I wasn't going to let him hold my hand. Kirk reached out to me and said, "Hand, hand!"

"No," I said. "Jump!"

But he refused.

I was feeling offended; how could he think that his dad would let him fall and hurt himself? I encouraged him to jump, but he continued to refuse. I kept urging him, wanting to see in him the attitude that said, "Dad, I believe you can and will catch me." I wanted him to demonstrate faith in me.

Through this silly little activity, God opened my eyes to how He feels when I fail to display faith in Him. The kind of faith God longs to see from His children is one that gives Him thanks, in advance, as we pray.

By the way, Kirk eventually took the risk and jumped, in faith, believing I would catch him. When he did that the first time, I held him close and said, "Kirk, I love you, and I would never let you fall." This is how your heavenly Dad feels toward you.

Kirk also discovered that "leaping with faith" was a lot more fun than holding on to control. The same is true of our faith in God as expressed in our giving thanks in advance.

3. Giving thanks is a form of worship.

In Luke 17, we read of an episode in the life of Jesus that shows how giving thanks is an expression of worship.

> While He was on the way to Jerusalem, He was passing between Samaria and Galilee. As He entered a village, ten leprous men who stood at a distance met Him; and they raised their voices, saying, "Jesus, Master, have mercy on us!"
>
> When He saw them, He said to them, "Go and show yourselves to the priests." And as they were going, they were cleansed.

> Now one of them, when he saw that he had been healed, turned back, glorifying God with a loud voice, and he fell on his face at His feet, giving thanks to Him. And he was a Samaritan.

> Jesus answered and said, "Were there not ten cleansed? But the nine—where are they? Was no one found who returned to *give glory to God*, except this foreigner?" And He said to him, "Stand up and go; your faith has made you well." (Luke 17:11–19)

Only one leper turned back to say thanks, recognizing that he'd been healed by the power of God. And he was right to do so. It was the power of God that had healed him. He fell at the feet of Jesus, overwhelmed with gratitude.

It's virtually impossible for us to comprehend the effects of the disease of leprosy or the stigma it carried in that culture. To be *healed* of that! No wonder this man was overwhelmed with thanksgiving! We read that he glorified God (in worship) "with a loud voice." He certainly had reason to worship with a loud voice.

But Jesus was puzzled. What about the other nine who were healed? Where are they? Were there no other worshippers among those whom God had healed?

Just as God is thrilled when we express faith in Him, He's equally thrilled when we worship Him. Worship is an acknowledgment of who He is and the recognition of what He has done. Worship is giving credit where credit is due. When you give thanks, you acknowledge God for who He is, you recognize what He has done for you, and you assign credit where credit is due. This is worship. So celebrate thanksgiving every day.

4. Giving thanks changes our perspective.

Finding contentment in spite of challenging or difficult conditions and circumstances requires a unique perspective—it requires God's perspective. This is where the unexplainable really comes into play.

Consider Paul, for example, as he sat in prison awaiting trial and a possible death sentence. That was the difficult situation he was in as he wrote,

> I have learned to be content in whatever circumstances I am. I know how to get along with humble means, and I also know how to live in prosperity; in any and every circumstance I have learned the secret of being filled and going hungry, both of having abundance and suffering need. (Phil. 4:11–12)

How in the world could he be content in the midst of these circumstances?

The answer: Paul possessed God's perspective on his circumstances. To see this, we need to flip back to these words in Philippians 1:

> Now I want you to know, brethren, that my *circumstances* have turned out for the greater progress of the gospel, so that my imprisonment in the cause of Christ has become well known throughout the whole praetorian guard and to everyone else, and that most of the brethren, trusting in the Lord because of my imprisonment, have far more courage to speak the word of God without fear. (Phil. 1:12–14)

Paul believed he was exactly where God wanted him to be. The Romans didn't imprison him; God did. And as he sat in prison, Paul knew God was giving him an opportunity to have an influence he could have in no other way.

The soldiers assigned to Paul were from the praetorian guard—made up of three hundred of Rome's brightest and best soldiers. They served as personal protection for the emperor himself. They were in the innermost circle of Roman power. As they guarded their prisoner—two at a time, in four-hour shifts—what do you suppose Paul talked with them about? Paul's testimony for the gospel was the reason that the cause of Christ had "become well known throughout the whole praetorian guard and to everyone else," as Paul reported. The innermost circle of Roman power was hearing about Jesus. Moreover, Paul knew that other Christians were inspired by his example, and as a result, were boldly testifying about Jesus in their own sphere of influence.

Paul saw his circumstances through the eyes of God. Essentially, he wasn't being held captive by the Romans; they were being held captive to him. Therefore, he could give thanks to God for his circumstances. This perspective—made possible only by God—enabled him to be content.

I encourage you to find God in the midst of your circumstances, whatever they may be. Trust me, He is there. Ask Him to reveal Himself and the purposes for which He has you where you are. Gaining His perspective on your circumstances will enable you to celebrate thanksgiving every day. It will also enable you to experience a contentment that's unexplainable apart from God.

Celebrating thanksgiving every day is a powerful practice. To be reminded of God's past provision and protection brings hope as we face the uncertainty of the future. And demonstrating our faith with a heart of worship honors God in the greatest of ways.

To gain God's perspective on the conditions and circumstances of life brings both encouragement and direction. In the end, giving thanks enables us to experience an unexplainable-apart-from-God kind of contentment.

More Reasons for Gratitude

Some time ago, I came across a perspective-giving article that provided some amazing statistics about our world. It noted, for example, how 80 percent of the world's people live in substandard housing, 70 percent are unable to read, and 50 percent suffer from malnutrition.

If you're anything like me, seeing such statistics will cause you to give thanks after realizing a fuller picture of our world.

Think of it this way:

- If you live in a good home, have plenty to eat, and can read, you're a member of a very select group.
- If you have a good house and enough food, can read, and own a computer, you're among the very elite.
- If you woke up this morning with more health than illness, you're more fortunate than the million who will not survive this week.
- If you've never experienced the danger of battle, the loneliness of imprisonment, the agony of torture, or the pangs of starvation, you're ahead of five hundred million people in the world.
- If you can attend a church meeting without fear of harassment, arrest, torture, or death, you're fortunate. More than three billion people in the world can't.
- If you have food in the refrigerator, clothes on your back, a roof over your head, and a place to sleep, you're richer than 75 percent of this world.
- If you have money in the bank and in your wallet, and spare change in a dish someplace, you're among the top 8 percent of the world's wealthy.
- If your parents are still alive and married to each other, you're very rare, even in the United States.[2]

- If you hold up your head with a smile on your face and are truly thankful, then you're blessed. Because the majority can—but most do not.

Therefore … celebrate thanksgiving every day.

Discussion Questions

1. Looking back on your life, in what significant ways can you see God's hand of provision and protection? Be specific.

2. In what ways can you give thanks in advance for something you're facing currently, and thereby express faith in God?

3. What can you give God thanks for right now, and in this way worship Him?

4. Can you think of a specific illustration from your life where gaining God's perspective on a matter made all the difference in being able to give Him thanks?

6

CONTENTMENT'S FOURTH SECRET

Embrace God's Truth

Finally, brethren, whatever is true, whatever is honorable,
whatever is right, whatever is pure, whatever is lovely,
whatever is of good repute, if there is any excellence and
if anything worthy of praise, dwell on these things.

PHILIPPIANS 4:8

I was strolling through a local shopping mall with two of my kids not long ago when we saw a large sign outside one of the stores. In big, bold letters, it read:

SHOP NOW
BUY MORE
BE HAPPIER

I asked my kids if they thought that claim was true. They quickly responded, "No," but added that evidently the store owner thought some people would believe it.

Truth is, many do believe it. In fact, the retail advertising industry is based upon the believability of that claim. It's estimated that more than 200 billion dollars is spent each year pushing products, up from 125 billion just ten years ago. It's also estimated that the typical American sees a million commercials by age twenty. Moreover, shopping centers are now outpacing national parks as holiday destinations.

One PBS documentary noted that the average American parent spends six hours a week shopping and only forty minutes a week playing with his or her children.[3]

So apparently a significant number of people believe that shopping now and buying more will make them happier.

But are we happier?

The store's claim—and the affirming response from so many people— actually reveals something about our fundamental discontent with what we have. On a deeper level, it also says something about the impact that ideas planted in our minds can have upon us, especially when we choose to accept those ideas as true. On some level, we do believe we'll be happier if we have something more than we now have.

The advertising industry is working very hard and being paid handsomely to convince us that buying more will make us happier. They bombard our minds with information and ideas that stir our natural discontent with what we have.

The Power of Thoughts

The efforts—and effectiveness—of advertisers only point toward the truth of this wise old saying:

Sow a thought, reap an action.

Sow an action, reap a habit.

Sow a habit, reap a character.

Sow a character, reap a destiny.

It all begins with a thought. While the food channel would have us believe we are what we eat, and the fashion channel tells us we are what we wear, and the advertising and retail industries tell us we are what we own, the truth is that we are what we think about. "As he thinketh in his heart, so is he" (Prov. 23:7 KJV). We become a reflection of what we think about and choose to embrace as true. Thoughts are very real—and oh, so powerful! They precede and have great influence on our feelings.

Paul understood the power of thoughts, and therefore he writes these words in Philippians 4:8:

> Finally, brethren, whatever is true, whatever is honorable, whatever is right, whatever is pure, whatever is lovely, whatever is of good repute, if there is any excellence and if anything worthy of praise, dwell on these things.

Here he identifies eight criteria regarding what we choose to think about and embrace as true:

1. Whatever is *true*—in accordance with fact or reality; accurate.
2. Whatever is *honorable*—deserving of honor and respect.
3. Whatever is *right*—being in accordance with what is just, good, and proper; conforming to facts or truth; correct, straight, genuine, real.
4. Whatever is *pure*—unmixed with any other matter; free from moral fault or guilt.
5. Whatever is *lovely*—delightful for beauty, harmony, or grace; attractive.

6. Whatever is *of good repute*—being favorably known, spoken of, or esteemed.

7. That which is *excellent*—superior, eminently good, first-class.

8. That which is *worthy of praise*—deserving approval, commendation, value, merit.

Paul then delivers the punch line: "*Dwell on these things.*"

What kind of information is Paul referring to in making such a list?

God's truth is perhaps the only body of information and thought that meets all eight of these criteria. His truth—like nothing else—is completely true, honorable, right, pure, lovely, of good repute, excellent, and worthy of praise.

This leads us to the fourth secret that Paul learned for experiencing unexplainable contentment: *Embrace God's truth.*

A Dwelling Place for Truth

I love Paul's choice of words in the last line of this verse: "*Dwell* on these things." In other words, let God's truth take up residence within your mind.

The impact of doing so was best summarized by Jesus Himself when He said to those who chose to abide in His Word as His true disciples, "You will know the truth, and the truth will make you free" (John 8:32). This freedom Jesus refers to releases us from a long list of captors that often hold us hostage—including worry, fear, and discontent. Paul has learned a secret for finding contentment: Embrace God's truth, and let it take up residence in your mind. Doing so plays a significant role in setting us free from worry and discontent.

This is true because of what happens when we *fail* to embrace truth.

The opposite of truth is lies. And where do lies originate? Jesus said this about the Devil: "He was a murderer from the beginning, and does not stand in the truth, because there is no truth in him. Whenever he speaks a lie, he speaks from his own nature, for he is a liar and the father of lies" (John 8:44). As God is the truth the whole truth, and nothing but the truth, so the Devil is a liar. Jesus states unequivocally, "There is *no* truth in him."

What is the Devil's goal? Peter tells us: "Your adversary, the devil, prowls around like a roaring lion, *seeking someone to devour*" (1 Peter 5:8). The Devil is your adversary, and he's seeking to hold you in bondage to all that will destroy you. *Lies* are his primary weapon for placing you in such bondage. To the degree that you choose to accept his lies as true, you'll find yourself in some sort of bondage.

Consider his tactics and efforts with Eve way back in the beginning:

> Now the serpent was more crafty than any beast of the field which the LORD God had made. And he said to the woman, "Indeed, has God said, 'You shall not eat from any tree of the garden'?"

> The woman said to the serpent, "From the fruit of the trees of the garden we may eat; but from the fruit of the tree which is in the middle of the garden, God has said, 'You shall not eat from it or touch it, or you will die.'"

> The serpent said to the woman, "You surely will not die! For God knows that in the day you eat from it your eyes will be opened, and you will be like God, knowing good and evil." (Gen. 3:1–5)

It's important to note in the Devil's initial question to Eve he placed an emphasis on what God restricted—when in truth, God's word to Adam and Eve focused on all that He permitted. God had told Adam, "From any tree of the garden you may eat *freely*; but from the tree of the knowledge of good and evil you shall not eat" (Gen. 2:16–17). The Devil's deceit-filled distortion of God's words placed an emphasis on what they couldn't do: "Has God said, 'You shall not eat from any tree of the garden'?"

In Eve's response, she affirms God's words, but she also adds something. She says they were not even to "touch" the fruit of the Tree of Knowledge. But God had never said, "Don't touch it."

In fairness to Eve, it's important to note that God's word concerning what was permitted came to Adam before Eve was even created (Gen. 2:16–18). It's likely that Eve received God's instruction about the Tree from Adam, not from God Himself. Perhaps this provides insight for why the Devil sought to converse with Eve rather than Adam.

In response to Eve's answer, the Devil responded vehemently, "You surely will not die!" *God lied to you,* he was saying. *Why would He do that?* "For God knows that in the day you eat from it your eyes will be opened, and you will be like God, knowing good and evil."

Two conflicting claims. Who to believe?

Adam and Eve made the choice to accept the Devil's word as true, and to reject God's Word.

The tragic result:

- great shame (Gen. 3:7)
- broken fellowship with God (3:8)
- fear (3:10)
- blame (3:12–13; Adam blames Eve, and Eve blames the serpent)
- pain in childbirth (3:16)
- the ground is cursed (3:17)
- loss of eternal life (3:19)
- need for clothing to hide their shame (3:21)
- removal from the garden of Eden (3:23)

And to think it all began with a thought—a thought based on a lie.

Free from the Devil's Influence

Now consider how differently Jesus handled a similar type of conversation with the Devil:

> And the devil said to Him, "If You are the Son of God, tell this stone to become bread."

> And Jesus answered him, "It is written, 'Man shall not live on bread alone.'"

> And he led Him up and showed Him all the kingdoms of the world in a moment of time. And the devil said to Him, "I will give You all this domain and its glory; for it had been handed over to me, and I give it to whomever I wish. Therefore if You worship before me, it shall all be Yours."

> Jesus answered him, "It is written, 'You shall worship the Lord your God and serve Him only.'"

> And he led Him to Jerusalem and had Him stand on the pinnacle of the temple, and said to Him, "If You are the Son of God, throw Yourself down from here; for it is written, 'He will command His angels concerning You to guard You,' and, 'On their hands they will bear You up, so that You will not strike Your foot against a stone.'"

> And Jesus answered and said to him, "It is said, 'You shall not put the Lord your God to the test.'" (Luke 4:3–12)

The Devil presented Jesus with three temptations, each built upon a lie. In every case, Jesus' immediate response began with, "It is written," and He went on to quote God's truth. Because Jesus rejected the lies of the Devil and embraced God's truth, He was able to experience victory over temptation and maintain His freedom.

The result: "When the devil had finished every temptation, he left Him until an opportune time" (4:13).

Approximately three years later, Jesus said to His disciples, "I will not speak much more with you, for the ruler of the world is coming, and *he has nothing in Me*" (John 14:30). Jesus was referring to the Devil, and stating that he had had no influence on Him. This was the case because Jesus had never chosen to accept any of the Devil's lies as true.

Still Lying

Now what about you? Who are you listening to? Whose thoughts are you choosing to accept as true? The Devil will work night and day to convince you that his lies are accurate, because deception is his only weapon.

Let me list for you some of his most common lies:

- God doesn't answer prayer.
- God won't meet your needs.
- God won't forgive your sins.
- God won't continue to forgive your sins.
- God blesses other people, but not you.
- You'll never change. You'll never be able to overcome "that" temptation.
- You're a failure.
- God doesn't have a plan for your life.
- God doesn't have the power to solve your problem; and even if He had that power, He's not going to use it on your behalf.

- God doesn't know what to do; and even if He did, He wouldn't tell you.
- God won't speak to you.
- God won't heal you.
- God has far more important matters to attend to than the ones in your life.
- God wants to restrict you and in turn rob you of your fun in life. That's why He has so many commands.
- The Bible is outdated, irrelevant, and filled with many stories that are nothing more than fairy tales.
- Jesus isn't the only way to God.

Have you heard any of these? There are many more, but these are some he seems to use repeatedly.

Based on my experience, every lie he utters calls into question either God's power (what God can't do), God's wisdom (what God doesn't know), or God's goodness (what God refuses to do). The Devil works to undermine the truth about God's nature or the truth of His Word to us. He even tries to speak lies about you—your nature, your potential, your abilities, and your future—to make you feel that you're worthless in God's eyes as well as your own.

If you choose to dwell on any of these lies—or even worse, choose to accept them as true—you'll suffer from worry, discontent, agitation, frustration, discouragement, despair, depression, self-pity, self-condemnation, shame, fear, bitterness, resentment, hopelessness, and certainly discontent.

Ultimately, the Devil hopes you'll stop reading your Bible and discontinue praying. His hope is to cut you off from God and the very life that's found in Him.

And to think it all begins with what you think about. Remember again:

Sow a thought, reap an action.

Sow an action, reap a habit.

Sow a habit, reap a character.

Sow a character, reap a destiny.

Countering the Lies

You become what you think about. So choose to embrace God's truth.

Let me give you a few examples of God's truth in response to our Enemy's lies I listed earlier:

- "And my God will supply all your needs according to His riches in glory in Christ Jesus" (Phil. 4:19). God *will* meet your needs.
- "If we confess our sins, He is faithful and righteous to forgive us our sins and to cleanse us from all unrighteousness" (1 John 1:9). God *does* forgive sin.
- "This is the confidence which we have before Him, that, if we ask anything according to His will, He hears us. And if we know that He hears us in whatever we ask, we know that we have the requests which we have asked from Him" (1 John 5:14–15). God *always* answers prayer.
- "What then shall we say to these things? If God is for us, who is against us?" (Rom. 8:31). God is on your side, fighting *for you*.
- "For I am convinced that neither death, nor life, nor angels, nor principalities, nor things present, nor things to come, nor powers, nor height, nor depth, nor any other created thing, will be able to separate us from the love of God, which is in Christ Jesus our Lord" (Rom. 8:38–39). You belong to God, and *nothing* can take you away from Him.
- "Greater is He who is in you than he who is in the world" (1 John 4:4). God is far superior to the Devil.

So when a thought enters your mind, learn to ask, *Is this thought in keeping with God's truth?* If so, dwell on it; if not, label it as the lie that it is, then replace it with God's truth.

For Great Peace

Remember the sign we saw in front of the store? "Shop Now, Buy More, Be Happier." Do *you* think that claim is true?

Listen to the truth through Jesus: "Beware, and be on your guard against every form of greed; for not even when one has an abundance does his life consist of his possessions" (Luke 12:15).

The shop owner who put that sign in front of his store was proclaiming a lie. Many have chosen to believe it, and as a result ended up in bondage to debt, among other things. This bondage to debt serves to increase worry and fear and discontent. Some wonder if they'll ever be free from such bondage. And to think it all began with a simple thought—based on a lie.

But the results of embracing God's truth are life-changing. As the psalmist writes, "Those who love Your law have great peace, and nothing causes them to stumble" (Ps. 119:165).

Isaiah put it this way: "Thou wilt keep him in perfect peace, whose mind is stayed on thee" (Isa. 26:3 KJV).

For experiencing an unexplainable contentment, one of Paul's secrets was the embracing of God's truth: "Dwell on these things." So what are *you* thinking about? What are you choosing to accept as true? Who are you listening to? What lies is the Devil whispering in your ear?

If you want to know the peace that surpasses all comprehension—unexplainable contentment—then embrace God's truth.

Discussion Questions

1. What lies does the Enemy seem to repeatedly use on you? Try and identify at least three of these.

2. What impact does it have on you when you accept the Enemy's lies as true?

3. Identify a truth—a specific verse if possible—that combats each of the Enemy's lies that he repeatedly uses on you. (If you're discussing these questions in a small group, help one another in identifying these truths.)

7

CONTENTMENT'S FIFTH SECRET

Practice These Things

*The things you have learned and received and
heard and seen in me, practice these things,
and the God of peace will be with you.*

PHILIPPIANS 4:9

Many companies are recognized by the tagline in their advertising. Here are a few of those taglines; see if you can identify them:

"You deserve a break today."

"See what Brown can do for you."

"Have it your way."

"Don't just buy stuff; do stuff."

"Fly the friendly skies."

"You're now free to move about the country."

"There are some things money can't buy. For everything else, there's …"

(Need some help? McDonald's, UPS, Burger King, Radio Shack, United Airlines, Southwest Airlines, and MasterCard.)

If Paul were to put a tagline to the passage in Philippians we've been focusing on, he might have been the first to say, "Just do it!" Nike's familiar tagline would serve well to capture what Paul communicates as a summary in Philippians 4:9:

> The things you have learned and received and heard and
> seen in me, *practice these things*, and the God of peace will
> be with you.

Paul is reminding us that mere talk is cheap; you gotta walk your talk; practice makes perfect; the proof is in the pudding; there's a time to put up or shut up.

Paul says there's a time to act, and that time is now: *You've learned from me, received from me, heard from me, and observed me—now it's your turn to practice these things.* In other words, *Just do it!*

What are "these things" Paul refers to here? They're those things he has just written about, what I've called the secrets to finding contentment:

1. Rejoice in the Lord (Phil. 4:4).

2. Pray about everything (4:6–7).

3. Celebrate thanksgiving every day (4:6).

4. Embrace God's truth (4:8).

Each of these secrets captures a powerful truth related to finding contentment that doesn't depend on outward conditions and circumstances. Paul exhorts us to move these "secrets" from theory to life: *Practice* these things. As significant as these four truths are, they're virtually useless unless practiced. Simply learning about them isn't enough. Merely receiving them for the truths they are won't get it done. Just hearing about them won't change your life. Seeing them in someone else's life won't bring peace that surpasses comprehension. You must "practice these things"—this is the fifth secret.

Application, Not Information

My dad was a bricklayer by trade. He took pride in his work and fully believed the saying, "Any job worth doing is worth doing right." He was a craftsman who took the quality of his work seriously.

I remember as a teenager asking him how he first learned to lay brick. He told me how his father, also a bricklayer, first showed him how to make mortar (or mud, as it's commonly called). He went on to explain that he would build small walls and corners or squares in the driveway behind his house, using leftover bricks his dad had brought home from the job. After completing each "mini-construction" project, his father would critique his work and then together they would tear it down, and my dad would build it over again.

I asked him how many times he built those "practice walls."

He chuckled and said, "I lost count." Then he added, "There's only one way to learn how to lay brick, and that's to do it."

Isn't this true in virtually every area of life? Great musicians don't become great simply because they master music theory. Hours and hours of practice with their instrument is key. Great athletes don't simply study their sport and its fundamentals; they get out on the field or court and practice until their muscles memorize the needed movements so they can do them without thinking. Talk to master chefs and ask where they learned to cook, and you'll hear them say, "In the kitchen." You don't become a master chef by reading recipes.

Progress in the realm of the Spirit is no different; it takes practice. *Rejoicing in the Lord* is nothing more than a nice, spiritual-sounding idea until you do it. It's when you do it that you experience the life of God being infused into your soul.

Praying about everything is nothing more than a comforting thought until you do it. It's only when you pray that you experience the peace that surpasses all understanding.

Celebrating thanksgiving every day is just a warm and uplifting thought until you practice it, at which time you discover its power to alter your perspective and attitude toward life.

And *embracing God's truth* is nothing more than wise counsel until you actually do it—and discover for yourself what Jesus meant when He said, "The truth will set you free."

It's important to note that Paul doesn't say, *"Learn and receive* these things and the God of Peace will be with you." No, he says, *"Practice* these things and the God of Peace will be with you." You have to do it.

So why don't we just do it?

For most of us, the explanation or excuse is lack of time. If you're like me, you're already trying to figure out how to squeeze thirty-six hours of life into each day. Time's a real issue—and yet, if we're completely honest with ourselves, we would have to admit we make time for what we genuinely believe is important.

It has been said before, and I believe it to be true: If you want to know what matters to you, take a look at your calendar and your checkbook. Time and money, two of our most treasured resources, flow to that which matters most to us.

If we were suddenly given thirty-six-hour days, most of us would try and squeeze forty-eight hours of life into them.

So the question must be asked: How important is it for you to experience God's unexplainable contentment? Given the conditions and the circumstances of your life, just how great is your need for peace that surpasses all comprehension? To what degree are worry and anxiety and stress and agitation and discontent strangling the joy of life right out of you? How badly do you want to be able to say, "I've learned to be content in any circumstance"? Do you long to be content?

If so, "practice these things, and the God of Peace will be with you."

This "peace of God" is different from the peace we find in the world. Jesus said, "Peace I leave with you; My peace I give to you; *not as the world gives* do I give to you. Do not let your heart be troubled, nor let it be fearful" (John 14:27). The peace the world offers depends on outward circumstances. When the conditions and circumstances of life are good and pleasing, we're at peace. And when they're not, we're not. This isn't God's peace. God's peace generates contentment in spite of circumstances. "Practice these things," and you'll know such peace.

Unexplainable Strength

At this point, I'm guessing you might like to say to me, "But you don't know *my* situation. My issue isn't time; it's energy." You want to know where you can find the strength, the power, the motivation to "practice these things." You feel as though your tank is nearly empty. You're just trying to hang on and make it through the day.

Paul, in anticipation of such thinking and feeling, adds a very significant truth to the formula in Philippians 4:13: "I can do all things *through Him who strengthens me."* Paul has discovered that God not only provides peace and contentment, but the strength we need when ours is gone. This strength is also unexplainable apart from God. And it flows to us as we step out to "practice these things."

Let me illustrate through the lives of my friends Dave and Cindy Siegers. On Saturday, June 16, 2007, Dave and Cindy experienced every parent's worst nightmare when their sixteen-year-old son Kyle was killed in a car accident. If life can deal a greater blow than the death of a child, I don't know what it is.

Kyle, like most sixteen-year-olds, was full of life. He had what could be called a huge personality—boisterous, loud, brash, bordering on cocky. He starred on the basketball court and football field as the kind of athlete who wanted the ball in his hands when the game was on the line. An abundance of friends made the Siegers' home a place of nonstop noise and action. Dave and Cindy obviously adored their son and found supporting him in his many involvements to be one of the great joys of life.

Then all of a sudden, in the blink of an eye, Kyle was gone. It's impossible to state with words the pain and heartache of such a loss. I'm convinced that the only ones who can truly understand are those who have suffered the same.

In the days, weeks, and months following Kyle's death, Dave and Cindy faced the same decision we all face when life strikes us a severe blow: Will we run *from* God, or run *to* God? In such cases, we want to find something or someone on whom to place blame. For many, God becomes the one who's blamed. *Why didn't He intervene? Why didn't He prevent this from happening?* Those who place the blame at God's feet usually end up running from Him. It's virtually impossible to embrace someone who on some level we blame for causing or allowing the suffering.

In Dave and Cindy's case, it became very clear from the earliest moments that they were going to run *to God*. In the past year and a half, as I've journeyed with them and watched them—sometimes up close and other times at a distance—I've found myself shaking my head in amazement. They've walked through the valley of the shadow of death, as David called it, and done so in a way that's unexplainable apart from God.

Even as I write of them, I find it difficult to explain how they've continued on as they have. While their pain is beyond description, they haven't retreated into grief and self-pity. Instead they've reached out in humility to love others and be loved by others in return.

It has been a hard road to travel, obviously the most difficult they've ever walked. They haven't denied their grief, nor have they hid it from others. At the same time, their humility and strength, their sense of conviction and purpose and calling, as well as the hope they've displayed, are all, frankly, unexplainable apart from God.

How has this been possible, given their loss?

At the risk of sounding overly simplistic, I can tell you they have "practiced these things." They've run into the arms of God. It's there that they've found the strength to move forward and continue to "practice these things."

They're learning and experiencing more than ever what it means to *rejoice in the Lord*. They cling to the conviction that their son is in the presence of God and to the hope that they'll spend an eternity with him and all those who call upon the name of Jesus. This is reason for rejoicing. They hold to the promise that nothing, not even death, can separate them from the love of Christ. This is reason for rejoicing. They see life through a different lens now; a lens that opens into eternity. As a result, they live with a different perspective on the here and now. They rejoice over that which cannot be taken away from them.

They're also learning to *pray about everything* as never before. As Cindy wrote recently, "I have seen God's hand in my life and the lives of others more this past year than any other year in my life." They've not only prayed on a new level, but they've asked others to pray on their behalf. On a regular basis, Cindy sends out email updates to a host of prayer partners. In humility, they've asked for support. God has answered these many prayers. They can feel His strength.

Celebrating thanksgiving every day is a tough one for them. Yet here, too, I've seen them "practice these things." On numerous occasions Dave has told me of the increasing number of opportunities he has had to share his faith in Jesus. He has said more than once, "I don't know if the same opportunities were there before and I just didn't see them, or if they have come now because I have something to share." For these opportunities, he's giving thanks. And on a very profound level, they give thanks for documents in Kyle's handwriting that testify of his faith in Jesus as his Savior. This is reason to give thanks and it can never be taken away.

Finally, I've watched them *embrace God's truth* with both arms. We're never more susceptible to the lies of the Devil than when we're experiencing times of trial. In such times, the Enemy mutters, "God doesn't love you"; "God doesn't care about you"; "God doesn't have the power to change your circumstances, and even if He did, He won't"; "You don't deserve His help—not someone like you." Blah, blah, blah, he babbles on and on, lie after lie. He would seek to tell Dave and Cindy, "Your life's over." While it's true that their life will never be the same this side of heaven, it's not over. I've watched Dave and Cindy resist the Devil's lies and embrace God's truth.

Dave and Cindy Siegers are unexplainable apart from God. And because of this fact, they're pointing others to God. Other people want to know how and why they've been able to continue on as they have. The only explanation: God. He wants all of us to possess a kind of contentment in spite of our outside conditions and circumstances, so that others see Him in us.

Abundance

So what are *your* circumstances? Chances are they aren't all that you'd like them to be. How do they impact your contentment?

God doesn't want you to go through life with a knot in your stomach. Jesus said, "I came that they may have life, and have it abundantly" (John 10:10). This abundance He speaks of is an inside job, first and foremost. It comes, for example, in the form of peace and contentment in spite of difficult circumstances. God wants to give you that peace and contentment because He loves you.

And when you receive it, you become unexplainable apart from Him. Like Dave and Cindy Siegers, you'll point others to Him. This is what God created you to do.

So do you possess an unexplainable-apart-from-God contentment? A contentment that surpasses and overcomes the outward conditions and circumstances of life? Such contentment is available if you learn the secrets:

Rejoice in the Lord.

Pray about everything.

Celebrate thanksgiving every day.

Embrace God's truth.

So *practice these things*, and *you* will know the peace of God that surpasses all comprehension … the peace that produces a contentment that's unattainable and unexplainable apart from God.

Discussion Questions

1. What grade (A, B, C, D, F) would you give yourself concerning "practicing these things" in the following areas:
    —rejoicing in the Lord
    —praying about everything
    —celebrating thanksgiving every day
    —embracing God's truth
2. What practical steps can you take to improve your grades in "practicing these things"?

PART TWO

UNEXPLAINABLE SUCCESS

Lifeshift 2: From Temporal to Eternal

8

WHEN SUCCESS
RESULTS IN FAILURE

*What will it profit a man if he gains the
whole world and forfeits his soul? Or what
will a man give in exchange for his soul?*

MATTHEW 16:26

Do you want to be a success?

Of course you do, we all do. No one gets up in the morning intending
to be a failure. No student enrolls in a class hoping to get an F. No athlete
enters the field of play with a heart set on losing. No one launches a career
with an eye toward crashing it. No one starts a business with the goal of going
belly-up. No one walks down the aisle to say "I do" with the hope of getting
divorced.

While some believe that the pursuit of success is evil, the truth is that
God Himself has given you a desire to succeed. Furthermore, He instructs
us in His Word to actually pursue success with all our hearts.

"Do you not know," Paul says, "that those who run in a race all run, but only one receives the prize? *Run in such a way that you may win*" (1 Cor. 9:24). He also writes, "Whatever you do, do your work heartily" (Col. 3:23). This command for wholehearted pursuit applies whether the arena is the classroom, the athletic field, the marketplace, the ministry, the management of money, or the building of relationships. There's not only nothing wrong with pursuing success; it's exactly what God tells us to go after: *Run to win. Whatever your endeavor, work at it with all your heart.*

What Is Success?

Here's the deeper issue we need to address: What *is* success?

In the world, success is almost always defined and measured by numbers. Businesspeople achieve the label "successful" based on the amount of dollars they generate. Coaches and athletes are successful based on how many wins or championships they accumulate. The successful student is the one with a high GPA or test score.

These numbers, regardless of the arena, are then translated into the world's ultimate measure of success—money. "Successful" businesspeople make big money. Likewise the "successful" coach or athlete is rewarded with the big bucks; remember the now-famous line "Show me the money" in the movie *Jerry Maguire*? And it's the "successful" student who earns the academic scholarship to attend college.

In the world, money and success go hand in hand. And it's here that a potential conflict arises, one that Jesus directly addresses: "No one can serve two masters; for either he will hate the one and love the other, or he will be devoted to one and despise the other. You cannot serve God and wealth" (Matt. 6:24). Jesus doesn't say we won't *try* to serve two masters; but He lets us know it can't be done.

If you're pursuing success, that's good. Hopefully you're pursuing it with all your heart. Now the question is, *what* success are you pursuing?

And even more importantly, *for what purpose?* In the end, what's the point of your achieving success? What's the target? When you come to the end of your life and look back in reflection, what sort of success will really matter?

The Wrong Pursuit

In Luke 12, we read of an encounter between Jesus and a young man that speaks directly to this matter of success. Jesus is talking with His disciples when suddenly a man from the crowd approaches Him and makes this request: "Teacher, tell my brother to divide the family inheritance with me" (Luke 12:13).

This man has a dilemma. Apparently his older brother isn't giving him his fair share of their father's estate. The man wants Jesus to tell his brother to pony up.

Jesus responds,

> "Man, who appointed Me a judge or arbiter over you?"
> Then He said to them, "Beware, and be on your guard
> against every form of greed; for not even when one has
> an abundance does his life consist of his possessions."
> (12:14–15)

While Jesus could have intervened to resolve this man's dilemma, He didn't choose to do so. I believe Jesus responded as He did because He knew the situation as this man described it was not the real issue. The real issue was greed. Jesus, knowing this, doesn't choose to address the symptom; He goes after the root problem—the mistaken belief that his life would be significantly better if he just got his portion of the estate. Jesus wanted to open his eyes not only to the greed in his heart, but to the lie that gave way to greed.

To make His point clear, Jesus went on to tell the following parable:

> The land of a rich man was very productive. And he began reasoning to himself, saying, "What shall I do, since I have no place to store my crops?" Then he said, "This is what I will do: I will tear down my barns and build larger ones, and there I will store all my grain and my goods. And I will say to my soul, 'Soul, you have many goods laid up for many years to come; take your ease, eat, drink and be merry.'"

> But God said to him, "You fool! This very night your soul is required of you; and now who will own what you have prepared?" (12:16–20)

Here we have a farmer who would no doubt be labeled as successful. He owned highly productive land and was therefore wealthy. The crops his land produced were so great that he'd run out of storage room. He decided to tear down his current barns and build bigger ones. In addition, he'd apparently achieved financial independence and was ready for early retirement. His 401(k) was so great, he need never work again. It was time to relax and take life easy.

But suddenly the farmer faced the end of everything. His time had come to die! And in the presence of God, the label he received was not "Successful," but *You fool!*"

By way of final application, Jesus states this conclusion: "So is the man who stores up treasure for himself, and is not rich toward God" (12:21). That rich farmer, Jesus is saying, was a fool because he spent his life pursuing the wrong kind of success.

Foolishness Exposed

Breaking down this parable, we observe this man's foolishness in at least three ways.

First, *his pursuit of success was all about himself.* He was the center of his world. In verses 17–19, he used a first-person pronoun eleven times. He was all about "I" and "my"—what *I* did with *my* stuff for *my* benefit.

He was deceived in believing that he was the cause and the source of his own abundance. He mistakenly saw himself as the owner: "my barns," "my grain," "my goods." He "stored up treasure *for himself,*" as Jesus expressed it.

If your pursuit and achievement of success begins and ends with you—your pleasure, your fame, your enjoyment, your recognition—you're spending your one and only life aiming at the wrong target. You're climbing a ladder that's leaning against the wrong wall. And sadly, you'll end up like this farmer in Jesus' parable.

Second, *this rich farmer's pursuit of success was focused solely on material things.* Of all that he attained and accumulated, how much did he leave behind when he died? *All* of it! How much did he take with him into eternity? *None* of it! As Jesus states so clearly, "What will it profit a man if he gains the whole world and forfeits his soul?" (Matt. 16:26). This farmer, so wealthy in the eyes of the world, was flat broke in the eyes of God. What a tragedy, and what a fool!

If your pursuit of success ultimately ends with "Show me the money," you're focused on the wrong thing. You may be hitting the world's bull's-eye—but, so what? It's the wrong target. What will you leave behind? Everything! What will you take with you into eternity? Nothing! Once again, you'll end up like the farmer.

Third, *his attainment of success was temporary.* Because his success was reflected in material things and aimed at his own pleasure, it came to an end when he came to an end. Worldly success doesn't last; it can't last.

Hence, the rhetorical question God asks this man on the night he was appointed to die: "And now who will own what you have prepared?" *It's not yours anymore; it's gone! Everything you worked for is gone!* God calls him a fool because only a fool would spend his one and only life pursuing and accumulating that which will one day be taken away.

God wants you to pursue, with all your heart, the kind of success that lasts forever. The right kind of success, the only kind worthy of pursuit, is eternal in impact. It's this success that makes a person rich toward God.

To pursue success that's eternal in impact will require a shift in focus. This is the second lifeshift I want to address—from *temporary* success to *eternal* success. If you don't want your end to be like that of the farmer in Jesus' parable, this lifeshift is a requirement. You'll need to define success differently than the world does. You'll need to set your sights on a new and different target.

This Won't Be Easy

Before we look at this new target, let me warn you: This shift won't be easy. You live in a world that's built upon, structured around, and all about material success. Every day you are bombarded from every side with messages promoting material success. The world's target is flashed before your eyes constantly.

This shift is made even tougher by the fact that our flesh is drawn toward material success. This is because our flesh craves control and comfort—exactly what material success is offering. This pull toward material success and the control and comfort it offers is so strong that Jesus said, "Truly I say to you, it is hard for a rich man to enter the kingdom of heaven. Again I say to you, it is easier for a camel to go through the eye of a needle, than for a rich man to enter the kingdom of God" (Matt. 19:23–24). The enticement toward material success is so powerful that many are unable to make the shift. Tragically, such people will one day appear before God and hear Him say, "You fool! This very night your soul is required of you; and now who will own what you have prepared?"

Paul speaks of a "lifeshift" in Romans 12:2: "And do not be conformed to this world, but be transformed by the renewing of your mind, so that you may prove what the will of God is, that which is good and acceptable and perfect." If you want to carry out God's will, this "success lifeshift" is one you'll need to make. And as you do, you'll find yourself entering the realm of the unexplainable apart from God. As your mind is being renewed, you'll begin to think in new ways. Having a new target—being rich toward God—will dramatically alter your life's goals and objectives. You'll embrace new values and set new priorities. You'll find yourself making decisions the world finds unexplainable.

Then, and only then, will your life truly point to God.

In the next several chapters we'll explore God's definition of success and discover what it means to be "rich toward God." So if you're ready, turn the page, and let's begin the lifeshift from temporary to eternal success.

Discussion Questions

1. What were you raised to believe about the definition of success in life? How have you been influenced by this understanding of success?

2. How do you define success in life today? Be as specific and practical as possible.

3. What is your personal "takeaway" from Jesus' parable in Luke 12 about the farmer? How will the message of this parable impact the way you live? Be specific and practical.

9

GOD SAYS: "BE FAITHFUL"

His master said to him, "Well done, good and faithful
servant. You have been faithful over a little; I will set
you over much. Enter into the joy of your master."

MATTHEW 25:21 ESV

The Bible clearly states that for each of us the day will come when we stand before God. What do you suppose He'll say to you? Based on the way you're spending your life, what would He have reason to say?

While I don't presume to know the answer to that for you or even for me, I can state with confidence something of what I know God wants to say to us.

A Parable of Encouragement
The words God wants to speak to us are found within Jesus' parable of the talents.

> For it will be like a man going on a journey, who called
> his servants and entrusted to them his property. To one he

gave five talents, to another two, to another one, to each according to his ability. Then he went away.

He who had received the five talents went at once and traded with them, and he made five talents more. So also he who had the two talents made two talents more. But he who had received the one talent went and dug in the ground and hid his master's money.

Now after a long time the master of those servants came and settled accounts with them. And he who had received the five talents came forward, bringing five talents more, saying, "Master, you delivered to me five talents; here I have made five talents more."

His master said to him, "Well done, good and faithful servant. You have been faithful over a little; I will set you over much. Enter into the joy of your master."

And he also who had the two talents came forward, saying, "Master, you delivered to me two talents; here I have made two talents more."

His master said to him, "Well done, good and faithful servant. You have been faithful over a little; I will set you over much. Enter into the joy of your master."

He also who had received the one talent came forward, saying, "Master, I knew you to be a hard man, reaping where you did not sow, and gathering where you scattered no seed, so I was afraid, and I went and hid your talent in the ground. Here you have what is yours."

But his master answered him, "You wicked and slothful servant! You knew that I reap where I have not sown and gather where I scattered no seed? Then you ought to have invested my money with the bankers, and at my coming I should have received what was my own with interest. So take the talent from him and give it to him who has the ten talents. For to everyone who has will more be given, and he will have an abundance. But from the one who has not, even what he has will be taken away. And cast the worthless servant into the outer darkness. In that place there will be weeping and gnashing of teeth." (Matt. 25:14–30 ESV)

Jesus told this particular parable while informing His followers about the end times. He sought to encourage them to live in such a way as to hear God say, "Well done, good and faithful servant. You have been faithful over a little; I will set you over much. Enter into the joy of your Master!"

When you appear before God, to hear such words from Him would scream "Success!" What will be required of you to hear such words?

Jesus answers this question through the parable, where the master represents God, and the servants—to whom the master's possessions (the talents) were entrusted—represent you and me. The specific scope of those entrustments varied, based on the differing abilities or capacities of the servants. But did you notice that the first two servants received the exact same commendation from their master, despite the difference in their "bottom-line" numbers?

This points out a stark difference between God's definition of success and the world's definition. In the ways of the world, the ten-talent servant would have received a far greater commendation than the four-talent servant, since the world defines success in numbers. The world asks, "Who sold the most? Who contributed the most? Who generated the most? Who scored the most? Who won the most? Who made the most?" God on the other hand measures *faithfulness*. He asks, *What did you do with whatever you were given?*

Due to being found unfaithful, the one-talent servant had his talent taken from him and given to the servant with ten. This servant suffered the consequences of unfaithfulness.

Let me pause and ask: What are you doing with what God has entrusted to you? Forget about what God has entrusted to someone else. All comparison with others is irrelevant. What are *you* doing with what God has given *you?*

If you're a bit confused about what God has given you, let me suggest a brief list (yours may be slightly different, but you'll get the idea):

- *natural talents* such as skilled hands, a voice to sing, an ear for music, the ability to play an instrument, coordination to dance, athletic ability, or the ability to write well, draw well, or speak effectively in front of a group of people
- *spiritual gifts*—all those who have a relationship with Jesus, as members of His body, have at least one spiritual gift according to New Testament passages like 1 Corinthians 12:7–11
- *financial resources*
- *material possessions* such as a home and a car and probably much more
- an *intellect,* and an *education* that helped develop it
- a *job* … perhaps a business you own or run
- *interests and passions* in such areas as music, art, sports, cooking, or a particular hobby

- *a kingdom passion*—a particular heart for some group of people or dimension of God's work
- *service opportunities* such as participating in a mission project or serving on the board of a faith-based or nonprofit organization or ministry, or volunteering at church

You've been given a great deal. What are you doing with all that God has given you?

Enjoyment versus Investment

In regard to all that we've been given, the world tells us to pursue, accumulate, and steward for our own benefit and enjoyment. The world tells you to think of yourself as an owner, just as the farmer did in the parable Jesus told in Luke 12. He spoke of "*my* barns … *my* grain … *my* goods"; the world teaches us to think in terms of *my* talents, *my* interests, *my* education, *my* resources, *my* home, *my* car. *And because I'm an owner, I have the right to use it all for my own benefit and enjoyment.*

Our ultimate objective becomes the same as it was for the farmer, who told himself, "You have many goods laid up for many years to come; take life easy, eat, drink, and be merry." The farmer possessed an "enjoyment perspective." His bottom line: *The ultimate goal of life is personal enjoyment, and material success makes that enjoyment possible.*

The world fails to see that life isn't ultimately found in enjoyment, but rather in *investment.* How different would this farmer's appearance before God have been, and how different the words he heard, had he spent his life investing what God had given him to help others on God's behalf.

It's true that God wants His children to enjoy what He has supplied. Paul reminds us (in 1 Timothy 6:17) that God "richly supplies us with all things to enjoy." But life doesn't climax or conclude there. You've been given what you have for the purpose of investment for the Master. You're a manager of what God owns. He has given you a portion of his portfolio to manage—to invest—on His behalf.

So again I ask, what are you doing with what God has entrusted to you? If your answer is, "I'm trying to make my life as comfortable and enjoyable as possible," you're likely to hear what the farmer heard when he appeared before God: *"You fool!* This very night your soul is required of you; and now who will own what you have prepared?"

How sad, how tragic, how devastating it would be to hear such words! What level of worldly success would mean anything at such a time?

This is why Jesus gave the instructions He did concerning the end times. He sought to encourage His followers to live their lives with an "investment perspective," so that when they appear before God they will hear, "Well done, good and faithful servant." This is God's will for you. It's with this perspective that you'll make your way into the realm of the unexplainable.

When you see yourself as a manager rather than an owner, you steward what you have differently. When you truly understand that you'll appear before God and give an account for how you've spent your life, you approach life differently. When you understand that life's ultimate goal isn't your enjoyment, but rather God's glory, you set different priorities and embrace different values. You'll spend money differently and use possessions for new purposes. Your talents and the opportunities before you take on new purpose and meaning. Even the way you spend your time will change. You'll see your involvements through a different lens.

You'll be "transformed by the renewing of your mind, so that you may prove what the will of God is," as Paul said in Romans 12:2. The only explanation for this transformation will be God. This is exactly the way it should be.

How Much Do We Keep?

Let me illustrate what I mean through the lives of my friends Ed and Dimple Owens.

Ed became a Christian in 1991 at the age of thirty-one. Some personal trials put him in a place of brokenness that caused him to be receptive to the message of Jesus Christ. Up to that point in his life, his only consideration of God occurred twice a year when he attended church on Christmas and Easter. Apart from those two holidays, God never even appeared on the radar of his life. But upon hearing the gospel and seeing his need for salvation, he gave his life to Jesus.

The sincerity of this decision became evident as he sought to grow in this newfound relationship.

As for his career, Ed was a money manager, and he'd experienced a measure of financial success. Based on lifestyle choices, he clearly possessed an enjoyment perspective toward life.

In 1996, he started his own company with the launching of a hedge fund. Almost immediately, his efforts were blessed with financial increase. He began making lots of money, far more than he needed to meet the wants and needs of his family.

For the first time in his life, he began to grapple with what it meant to honor God with his finances. Up to this point in his life, all he'd ever been taught and known was based upon an enjoyment perspective. In fact, that's why he chose the career he did. Now, his perspective was changing.

He and Dimple began giving 10 percent of their income to the work of God's kingdom. This giving represented a change, but frankly had little impact on them, since the remaining 90 percent was substantial. They drove nice cars, wore nice clothes, ate at nice restaurants, and vacationed at nice places where they stayed in the nicest hotels.

While they also lived in a nice home, they clearly had the money for an even nicer one. They identified five acres of property in an exclusive and isolated area and spent two years designing and building their dream home. Ed told me recently of how he walked the property prior to purchasing it, wanting to make sure that he could hear nothing as he stood upon it.

Upon completion, they furnished their dream abode with the finest goods money could buy. At the same time, they still could afford to increase their giving to approximately 25 percent of their income. In fact, there was so much left over, they purchased a second home. While they didn't use it much, they justified having it by letting others use it free of charge as a kind of "retreat center." Many of those who did so were people in vocational ministry who were otherwise unable to afford such places.

Ed's business continued to flourish, and he and Dimple continued to grapple with what it meant to honor God with their resources. Their giving increased. They sincerely sought God's definition of generosity. They decided to start a charitable foundation and placed 50 percent of their annual income into it.

At the encouragement of a friend, Ed read the New Testament from start to finish, making note of every verse that said something about money or possessions. They listened to Bible teachers such as Randy Alcorn and John Piper, and humbly submitted themselves to the instructions being given.

In time, Ed and Dimple came to the conclusion that they'd been asking the wrong question about money and giving. They decided the right question wasn't *How much are we to give?* but rather *How much are we permitted to keep?*

For the first time, they truly understood their role as managers of what God owned. They began to see that God's perspective toward money included not only generosity toward others but frugality toward self.

God's Business

At this point, Ed and Dimple truly entered the realm of the unexplainable apart from God. Generosity itself isn't really unexplainable; there are many people, including those who don't claim to be under God's influence, who display generosity. They give large amounts of money to worthwhile causes and are considered generous as a result. In most cases, however, this generosity is practiced while they continue to maintain an "enjoyment perspective" toward life. Their generosity has no significant impact on them personally.

But as Ed and Dimple began to see that God's will concerning money included not only generosity toward others but frugality toward self, they discovered significant, life-changing implications.

They felt led by the Lord to sell their dream home after living in it for just four years. They also sold their "retreat center" and several cars that weren't really needed. They made these decisions in order to drastically reduce their expenses so they could give more to help others in the name of Jesus. They also established a budget, and Ed began meeting regularly with a pastor from his church for the sake of accountability to the budget.

Then in 2003, in the midst of all these personal changes, government regulations changed some of the laws governing hedge funds. The net effect was to put an end to Ed's hedge fund, resulting in the closing of his business. From 2004 through 2006, he received no income.

While some in similar circumstances may have been tempted to question God's goodness for allowing such events to unfold, in light of the decisions they were making, Ed and Dimple had no such thoughts. By this time, their perspective toward money, possessions, and the very purpose behind life had changed dramatically. They saw themselves not as owners but as managers of what God owned and entrusted to them. That hedge fund was God's business and God's money—and if He decided to bring it to an end, that was His right.

An investment perspective replaced the enjoyment perspective that had dominated their thinking and lifestyle choices for so long. Ed believed that God had given him an ability to make money and that God had done so as a means of meeting needs and putting His generosity on display. Ed and Dimple no longer focused on how much to give, but asked God how much to keep.

All these changes in their approach to life were unexplainable apart from God. In the eyes of the world, Ed and Dimple had lost their minds. There was no explanation for the choices they were making—apart from God. As a result, God has been put on display through them, which is exactly the purpose for which they were created.

Given their current life course, I would say there's a very good chance they're going to hear from the Lord someday, "Well done, good and faithful servant. You have been faithful over a little; I will set you over much. Enter into the joy of your Master." If this proves to be the case, they'll be classified as "rich toward God"—and a smashing success in ways that count for all eternity.

Worth Pondering

So what about you? Are you being faithful? What are you doing with what God has given you (i.e. natural talents, spiritual gifts, material possessions, etc.)? Do you see yourself as an owner or a manager? Do you possess an investment perspective toward all you have? For whose benefit and enjoyment are you spending your one and only life? What are you doing that will last forever?

These are questions worth pondering.

What a huge difference there is between hearing God say, "You fool! Who will own what you have prepared?" and hearing Him say, "Well done, good and faithful servant—enter into the joy of your Master!"

Discussion Questions

1. Were you raised with more of an "enjoyment perspective" or more of an "investment perspective" toward life? Explain.

2. If someone were to follow you closely for the next month, what would they conclude about your understanding of success and your perspective toward life?

3. Make a brief list of what God has given you that He now calls you to faithfully steward for His glory. (Identify at least five of these gifts.) What does being faithful with these things look like in everyday life? (Be specific and practical.)

4. What changes, if any, do you currently need to make in your life to be assured of hearing God say to you, "Well done, good and faithful servant"?

10

GOD SAYS: "BEAR FRUIT"

My Father is glorified by this, that you bear
much fruit, and so prove to be My disciples.

JOHN 15:8

Jesus once said to His disciples, "My Father is glorified by this, that you bear much fruit, and so prove to be My disciples" (John 15:8).

As we follow the flow of John's gospel, we find that Jesus spoke these words on the heels of the Last Supper, immediately preceding His time of prayer in the garden of Gethsemane. This timing gives these words additional significance, since they're some of the last He spoke before being taken away and crucified.

Jesus continued, "You did not choose Me but I chose you, and appointed you that you would go and bear fruit, and that your fruit would remain, so that whatever you ask of the Father in My name He may give to you" (15:16). The disciples clearly understood the analogy and the imagery these words conjured up, as vineyards dotted the countryside around them. They knew about vines, branches, and the grapes that grew from them. They understood the role of the vinedresser and the pruning process he used to increase the fruit. Now Jesus was telling them that *they* were the branches, and that they were to abide in Him—the vine—to bear fruit. "It's through fruit-bearing," Jesus was telling them, "that you put My Father on display and point others to Him." They were chosen and appointed for this purpose of bearing fruit.

What Is This Fruit?

What was true for Jesus' disciples back then is also true for Jesus' disciples today. And success in life, as defined by God, is tied directly to bearing fruit.

So what exactly is this fruit to which Jesus is referring?

The New Testament speaks of two kinds of fruit—the inner kind, which is the fruit of Christlike *character,* and the outer kind, the fruit of Christlike *influence.*

The inner kind of Christlike character is most clearly spelled out in Galatians 5:22–23: "The fruit of the Spirit is love, joy, peace, patience, kindness, goodness, faithfulness, gentleness, self-control." When the Holy Spirit manifests His presence in a person's life, these nine characteristics emerge, as they reflect the characteristics found in Jesus. And these nine characteristics are a big deal to God. While success in the eyes of the world begins and ends with what you do and accomplish, success in the eyes of God begins with *who you are.*

I came to a personal discovery of that truth in a profound way.

In the summer of 1992, I was graciously given the opportunity to take a four-month sabbatical. Sabbaticals are fairly common among professors and pastors who spend considerable amounts of time in study and preparation for the sake of presentation. In my case, it was intended for a little different purpose. Seventeen years earlier, I'd helped start Willow Creek Community Church in suburban Chicago and by God's grace had played a fairly significant role in its development. The rapid numerical growth of the church (to an attendance of approximately sixteen thousand), and the demands and pace brought on by that growth, had placed me near the edge of burnout. I was in clear need of a break.

Something else further complicated my situation: For some time I'd been sensing that my involvement with the church was coming to an end. Was this simply because I was nearing burnout? Or was God redirecting me? And if He was redirecting me, where did He want me to go and what did He want me to do?

In order to find answers, I needed some time alone with God.

At the very start of my sabbatical, I began to pray and ask God to reveal to me what He wanted me to do. I prayed fervently, off and on throughout each day, as I wanted a clear word of direction from Him. I tried to listen for an answer. I read the Bible, knowing that God speaks through His Word. I made lists reflecting the pros and cons of every potential option. In addition, I sought the counsel of people I respected and trusted, thinking that God might speak through one of them.

But after three months, what I was hearing from God could be summed up in one word—*silence.*

With only one month remaining in my sabbatical, I was more confused than ever. I was very open to returning to the staff of the church; in fact, doing so made all the sense in the world, as I had a family of five to support. However, I didn't want to do that just for the sake of a paycheck. I wanted the leading of God.

Finally, an Answer

Early into my fourth month, while driving alone in my car, I cried out to God with a voice of exasperation: "God, what do You want me to do?" His silence had been deafening, and I was running out of time.

What I then heard was this: "I don't really care what you do. I care about *who you are*—and who you are is failing." It wasn't an audible voice, but it was unmistakably clear. I received these words not as condemnation, but as an expression of mercy.

I returned to where I was staying and turned in my Bible to Galatians 5:22–23, verses I'd read countless times before. In fact, I had them memorized. This time, I read them more carefully and slowly than ever before.

Then I did something I'd never done before with these words. I began to evaluate myself in light of those nine characteristics on the list.

"*Love.* How am I doing?" I didn't score well, so I moved on.

"*Joy.* How's that going for me?" I didn't score well here, either, so I kept going.

"*Peace.* Hmm; I'm one of the most stressed-out people I know. And *patience.* Oh wow! I hate standing in line—any line, anytime, anywhere, for anything."

I kept moving through the characteristics, one by one, feeling worse by the minute. Finally, I came to *faithfulness*—and finally had opportunity to hold my head high. I *was* faithful. I never let a ball drop. I could spin a lot of plates at once.

Just as I was beginning to feel better about myself, I came to *gentleness,* where I bottomed out. With the exception of my family, few on planet Earth would have called me Gentle Don.

I completed my evaluation on a higher note with *self-control.* Personal discipline had always been somewhat of a strength for me.

In reflection, and perhaps due to all the baseball I'd played, I summed up my little self-evaluation with this thought: *I'm two for nine.* Though I had to admit that my two "hits" had little to do with the influence of the Holy Spirit. Based on family background and God-given temperament and personality, faithfulness and self-control came somewhat naturally to me. It was the other seven characteristics that pleaded for the influence of the Holy Spirit. In those areas, I was failing. And I knew it.

I then heard the voice of the Holy Spirit within: "If staying on staff at Willow Creek will help you become a more loving, joyful, peaceful, patient, kind, good, and gentle man, then stay there. If not, it's time to move on."

For three-plus months, I'd been asking God what He wanted me to "do," believing that His leading would come through "doing" something. After prolonged silence, He was finally speaking—not about what I was to do, but about who He wanted me to be.

I knew the culture at Willow Creek (I'd helped create it), and I knew that to succeed in bearing the fruit of Christlike character, I needed a new environment. At that moment, I made my decision to leave the staff of the church.

Instantly, I felt an overwhelming sense of peace come over me. I took this peace as God's affirmation that I'd just made the right decision.

As a result of this encounter with God, I made a rather unexplainable-apart-from-God decision to quit my job without having another one to go to. As an intensely practical individual, firmly committed to my God-given responsibility of providing for my family's needs, I cannot explain this decision, apart from God. In the eyes of some, it was irresponsible and foolish. But I had no anxiety about it. Looking back, I believe God by His grace gave me a confidence to believe that He was leading me.

As things turned out, He did provide—in every way.

After communicating my decision to resign, I called five friends—brothers in the Lord—and asked each if they would be willing to spend a day together with me to help me discern my potential next steps. Each agreed, so we gathered late in the fourth month of my sabbatical to seek God's further direction. By the end of our day together, a path was laid out for me, and I've basically been on it ever since.

I didn't realize it at the time, but I was about to enter God's pruning process, as Jesus describes when He said, "Every branch in Me that does not bear fruit, He takes away; and every branch that bears fruit, He prunes it so that it may bear more fruit" (John 15:2). While I would like to report that I'm now "nine for nine" when it comes to those fruit-of-the-Spirit qualities, that would be a stretch—in some cases a rather big stretch. I've had some serious ground to make up with regard to those other seven fruits. I can say, however, that God has taken me to a new place in my relationship with Him. While others may not always see my transformation, I do. I know what God has done and what He's continuing to do.

Who You Are

So what about you? Are you bearing fruit? What's your batting average?

Love—how are you doing?

Joy—do you have it?

Peace—are you experiencing it?

Patience—are you expressing it?

Are you *kind* toward others?

Is your heart increasing in *goodness*?

Are you being *faithful* with what has been entrusted to you?

Are you *gentle* in manner?

Do you exercise *self-control* in attitude, word, and deed?

Probably, like me, you can identify a few of the nine characteristics that come somewhat naturally to you, based on your makeup. But what about the remaining characteristics that require the influence of the Holy Spirit?

While the world cares almost exclusively about what you do and accomplish, God cares first and foremost about who you are. From His vantage point, everything starts there. He wants His presence to so fill your life that you experience the blessings that come from being a loving, joyful, peaceful, patient, kind, good, faithful, gentle, and self-controlled person.

This is success as He defines it—bearing much fruit. As Jesus said, "My Father is glorified by this, that you *bear much fruit,* and so prove to be My disciples." The world may not measure or value such marks of character, but God does. And the first kind of fruit He's looking to produce in you is the fruit of Christlike character.

To produce this fruit, God may lead you to make an unexplainable-apart-from God decision. He may put you through a pruning process that leaves you searching for explanation as to why you're going through all you are.

Trust me when I say that God produces the fruit of patience by placing us in circumstances that test our patience. In the same way, He produces love and gentleness by placing people in our lives who require both.

I've discovered that God's pruning process often seems unexplainable until it's completed, at which time His ways become clearer. In some cases, God may simply perform the unexplainable in you as a result of your abiding in Him. I know a pastor, for example, who's one of the kindest and most gentle people I've ever met. When I first heard his story of coming to know Jesus, I was shocked to learn that he once possessed a wild and violent temper. I couldn't believe it. *Impossible,* I thought; *not him.* But his wife affirmed it: "His temper was uncontrollable." How did he change so dramatically, so quickly? There was only one explanation: God did it!

God longs to do the unexplainable *in* you, out of His great love *for* you. And no one will benefit more from your bearing the fruit of Christlike character than you. God wants to produce this fruit in your life for *your* good, *your* benefit, *your* blessing. In this way, He displays Himself in you and thereby brings glory to His name.

This is success in His eyes—that you bear much fruit and so prove to be His disciple.

Discussion Questions

1. Of the nine characteristics listed as fruit of the Holy Spirit in Galatians 5:22–23 ("love, joy, peace, patience, kindness, goodness, faithfulness, gentleness, self-control"), which ones seem to come somewhat naturally to you as a reflection of your makeup and upbringing? Which ones will clearly require the influence of the Holy Spirit within?

2. To what degree and in what ways have you already experienced the influence of the Holy Spirit within you in terms of these nine characteristics?

3. Can you look at any current circumstances and see how the Holy Spirit is at work to bear the fruit of Christlike character in your life? Explain.

4. In personal response to these chapters (8, 9, and 10), complete this statement: *In my life, God is the only explanation for …*

11

GOD SAYS: "BEAR MORE FRUIT"

Every branch in Me that does not bear fruit, He
takes away; and every branch that bears fruit,
He prunes it so that it may bear more fruit.

JOHN 15:2

God wants to do the unexplainable not only *in* you, but *through* you. As I pointed out in the last chapter, the Holy Spirit's presence and influence within you produces the fruit of Christlike character. This "inner fruit" is the first of two kinds of fruit that God wants to bring forth from your life. The second is of the "outer" variety; I call it the fruit of Christlike influence.

Peter describes this influence in the simplest of terms in Acts 10:38: "You know of Jesus of Nazareth, how God anointed Him with the Holy Spirit and with power, *and how He went about doing good and healing all who were oppressed by the devil,* for God was with Him." With these brief words, Peter captures the essence of Jesus' influence.

When the Holy Spirit manifests Himself through you, the influence of God Himself is felt around you. The people you come in contact with will benefit. The world in which you personally travel will be impacted.

Christlike Influence

Earlier I told you the story of my friends Dave and Cindy Siegers, who lost their sixteen-year-old son, Kyle in an automobile accident in 2007. Just last week, Cindy sent an email to a number of us who pray for her and Dave.

Cindy had been traveling by plane with her mother on a long flight with multiple connections. On one leg of the flight, instead of being seated next to her mother, Cindy was seated next to a married couple, and she carried on an extended conversation with them. The couple, Sam and Mary, told Cindy that they'd been married for thirty-eight years, but their relationship seemed strained. As Cindy wrote in her email:

> About an hour or so into our flight, I mentioned Kyle's passing. Mary asked if it was a car accident. Her eyes appeared watery as she leaned over her husband to tell me that their daughter had been in an accident when she was sixteen. She was driving her newly purchased vehicle and making a left-hand turn when a car ran a red light and hit her car. I could hear the stress in Mary's voice.

Cindy told how her faith and Dave's faith had enabled them to endure after their son's death. Her conversation with the couple continued:

> Over time Mary asked me what my religion was, if I was angry with God, and what books I read. I answered her inquiries as best I could at the time. She told me that Sam

had lost his job two years ago and he was very angry. They come from a religious background but admittedly don't have much Bible knowledge.... I knew that my sitting by them was "God-appointed" and I asked them for their email address so that I could contact them when I returned home.

Was it just coincidence that Cindy sat next to this couple? I doubt it. God-appointed? Cindy believed so, and I agree. As it turns out, the seat next to her mother remained empty for the entire flight. God was reaching out to this hurting couple, and He was doing so through Cindy. By responding as she did, she was bearing the fruit of Christlike influence. She was doing as Jesus would have done had He been there in the flesh.

Doing Good

God wants you and me to bear much fruit, for His glory. How do we do this? By doing good—just as Cindy did, and as Jesus did, as Peter described in Acts 10:38: "He went about doing good."

As Jesus traveled through life, He engaged in doing good works. From the gospel accounts, we know that He fed the hungry, healed the sick, encouraged the discouraged, forgave the guilty, loved the unlovable, and taught all who longed for truth. The result of His doing good was always the same: Those on the receiving end were served, helped, lifted, encouraged—in a word, *blessed.* They often went away praising God.

As we travel through life, God wants to express Himself through us. He wants us to have an influence like that of Jesus.

The list of what this could include for you is almost endless. Let me help get you started:

- a word of encouragement to someone who needs or deserves it

- a smile and a kind word to someone who looks like they have the weight of the world on their shoulders
- a financial gift to someone who's coming up short
- the gifts of time and a listening ear to someone who could use both
- stopping to pray with someone who needs God's intervention on their behalf—perhaps desperately
- a note of encouragement or thanks to someone who would take either to heart
- setting up tables or providing food at the local mission
- volunteering to help out with child care at church
- donating goods or services to someone in need
- visiting someone in the hospital or shut in at home
- bringing a meal to a family going through a tough time

You get the idea. This isn't difficult stuff, and it doesn't need to be dramatic in delivery or effect. These simple expressions of "doing good" put the love, the kindness, the goodness, and the gentleness of God on display in a tangible way.

"For we are His workmanship," Paul tells us, "created in Christ Jesus for good works, which God prepared beforehand so that we would walk in them" (Eph. 2:10). God has created and designed us to carry out these good works on His behalf, as His representatives. Based on this verse in Ephesians, I like to think that God places a host of potential good works in my path every day. Then as I walk through my day, it's up to me to respond to each opportunity as a way of bringing God's presence and influence into the world.

It's also important to note what else Peter says about Jesus in Acts 10:38: "God anointed Him with the Holy Spirit and with power." Jesus was able to spot the good works in His path and to do them because of the presence and power of the Holy Spirit within Him.

That's why Jesus spoke these words to His disciples:

> Abide in Me, and I in you. As the branch cannot bear
> fruit of itself unless it abides in the vine, so neither can
> you unless you abide in Me. I am the vine, you are the
> branches; he who abides in Me and I in him, he bears
> much fruit, for apart from Me you can do nothing. (John
> 15:4–5)

We don't engage in good works merely like a good Boy Scout would. We engage in good works in response to the influence of the Holy Spirit upon us.

This explains why fruit-bearing begins on the inside with the fruit of Christlike character. As we abide in Jesus, and walk according to the Holy Spirit, we too are able to see the good works in our path and tap into the power of God to carry them out.

What sort of influence do you suppose God would have in our world if each and every one of us who call Him Lord would awake each morning and ask Him to open our eyes to the good works He was placing in our path that day? Our collective influence would be enormous as the presence of God was released in the world. The churches and spiritual communities of which we are a part would have an unexplainable-apart-from-God influence.

Healing Those Oppressed by the Devil

Now look with me at another phrase in Acts 10:38 that speaks of Jesus' influence: He went about "healing all who were oppressed by the devil."

Jesus was well aware of the influence of evil all around Him. Just a casual reading of the four gospels reveals that Jesus regularly encountered

people who were experiencing the effects of demonic influence. It's an ines-
capable fact that delivering people from demonic influence was a big part
of His ministry. And when He sent His disciples out to minister on His
behalf, He gave them authority over demons.

For example, we read that "He called the twelve together, and gave
them power and authority over all the demons" (Luke 9:1). In Luke's next
chapter, we read of seventy disciples Jesus sent out in pairs to conduct ministry, and how on their return they reported, "Lord, even the demons are
subject to us in Your name." Jesus responded, "I was watching Satan fall
from heaven like lightning. Behold, I have given you authority to tread
upon serpents and scorpions, and over all the power of the enemy, and
nothing will injure you" (Luke 10:17–19).

Delivering people from demonic influence was a normal and regular
part of Jesus' life. And the same was true of those He called and commis-
sioned to minister on His behalf.

So let me ask: What has changed since those days? Do we somehow
believe that the demons are gone? If so, how do we explain the presence of
evil all around us?

The Bible is clear in teaching that the Enemy is still present and very
much at work. Therefore, to bear the fruit of Christlike influence is to be an
agent of deliverance for those who are experiencing demonic influence.

What does this look like on a practical level?

I think of my friends Harry and Norine Pothoff, who lead a ministry called Families Victorious. Born out of this couple's own experience,
Families Victorious exists to deliver those who are caught in the grip of
addiction. Some thirty years ago, God delivered Harry from an addiction
to alcohol. Looking back on those days, Harry says, "For twelve years Satan
had his foot on my chest."

Today, he and Norine work full time helping those who are battling
the demon of addiction. And because God is anointing their efforts,

many are being set free. Harry and Norine are bearing the fruit of Christlike influence as they work to "heal those who are oppressed by the devil."

There are many other ways to be involved in healing those who are oppressed by the Devil. Let me mention a few:

- Helping someone escape the prison of resentment and bitterness as a result of choosing to forgive. The New Testament says clearly that an unforgiving spirit places a person under demonic influence (Matt. 18:21–35; 2 Cor. 2:9–11; Eph. 4:26–27; Heb. 12:14–15). Therefore, when you help people forgive those who have wronged them, you're serving as an agent of healing to those oppressed by the Devil. This is the fruit of Christlike influence.

- Providing support and accountability for someone who's otherwise falling repeatedly to the same temptation. In such a case, the Enemy has found a weakness in someone that he's exploiting and thereby gaining access for additional influence. When you help such a person experience lasting victory over that temptation, you're serving as an agent of healing to those oppressed by the Devil. This is the fruit of Christlike influence.

- Sharing the truth of God's Word with someone who's in bondage due to believing a lie. The Enemy is a liar, Jesus said, and whenever he speaks, he speaks a lie (John 8:44). Those who believe his lies in turn open themselves to his influence. When you help someone discover the truth of God's Word in a way that dispels a lie, you're serving as an agent of healing to those oppressed by the Devil. As Jesus said, "You will know

the truth, and the truth will make you free." This is the
fruit of Christlike influence.

- Helping someone make a life-choice that's in accordance
with God's will. In Galatians 6:7, we read, "Do not be
deceived, God is not mocked; for whatever a man sows,
this he will also reap." We experience the blessings and
consequences of our choices. Therefore, when someone
makes a choice in conflict with God's will, the results are
usually painful. If God's will isn't being done, then the
Enemy's will is. Carrying out his will is to bring us under
his influence. Therefore, when we help someone make a
choice that's in line with God's will, we're serving as His
agent in healing those oppressed by the Devil.

- Introducing someone to Jesus. This is the greatest and
ultimate form of deliverance. In Colossians 1:13 we
read, "For He rescued us from the domain of darkness,
and transferred us to the kingdom of His beloved Son."
There are only two kingdoms, and each and every one of
us is a member of one or the other. To lead someone into
a relationship with Jesus means a transfer of his or her
kingdom membership. There's no greater way to serve as
God's agent in healing those oppressed by the Devil than
by helping someone experience salvation through Jesus.

The fruit of Christlike influence is to do as Jesus did as He traveled
through life, just as Peter described it—doing good and healing those
oppressed by the Devil.

Are *you* bearing the fruit of Christlike influence? What "good works"
has God placed in your path today, or this past week? Did you see them?
Did you carry them out and, as a result, bring God's influence into your
world?

Is there any place where you're currently serving as God's agent of healing to those oppressed by the Devil? Who is He using you to deliver from the Devil, on His behalf?

The description of Jesus in Acts 10:38 captures the essence of His influence. To follow His example is to bear the fruit of Christlike influence. This is success in the eyes of God—that you bear much fruit and so prove to be His disciples.

Discussion Questions

1. What opportunities for "doing good" has God placed in your path in recent days? Explain what happened.
2. Can you identify any opportunities for "doing good" that you failed to act upon? Explain.
3. What is your response or reaction to this chapter's discussion about "healing those oppressed by the devil"?
4. Based on the examples this chapter provides, has God ever used you to help deliver someone from demonic influence?
5. Can you think of someone at the present time who may be experiencing demonic influence? How could God use you to help deliver them?

12

GOD SAYS: "EXPERIENCE MY JOY"

These things I have spoken to you so that My joy may
be in you, and that your joy may be made full.

JOHN 15:11

The apostle Paul penned approximately two-thirds of the New Testament over a period of nearly twenty years. In the very last chapter of his very last letter—written from a prison cell—we read these words:

> For I am already being poured out as a drink offering, and the time of my departure has come. I have fought the good fight, I have finished the course, I have kept the faith; in the future there is laid up for me the crown of righteousness, which the Lord, the righteous Judge, will award to me on that day; and not only to me, but also to all who have loved His appearing. (2 Tim. 4:6–8)

From these words, we can deduce that Paul knew his life on earth was nearing an end. He had been in prison before, but this time seemed different. He had the distinct impression that he wouldn't be getting out as before.

As a prisoner, he had many hours to reflect upon the past. I imagine him sitting back, taking a deep breath, then putting into written words what his heart was assured of: *I've fought the good fight … finished the course … kept the faith.…* These are words of victory, sentiments signaling success. So Paul continues: *There's laid up for me a crown.…*

His words convey an inner satisfaction and deep-seated fulfillment. He's like the marathon runner who has a comfortable lead with only a half mile to go. He can see the finish line. He knows he has won. He imagines the wreath being placed upon his head and the gold medal around his neck. His mind drifts back to all the training, all the miles he has logged, all the injuries he has overcome, all the aches and pains he has endured, all the setbacks, the days running alone, the inclement weather. And now, in this moment, he knows: It's all been worth it.

Perhaps Paul is recalling the words he wrote many years before, in a much earlier letter: "Do you not know that those who run in a race all run, but only one receives the prize? Run in such a way that you may win" (1 Cor. 9:24). He'd written these words as a younger man with many miles to go. Now as an old man, all those miles are behind him. He now knows he has won. He sits in prison in anticipation of looking into the eyes of Jesus Himself, who will present him with the crown of righteousness. He's clearly looking forward to that day.

In this final letter, we get a glimpse into the soul of a man who has experienced, and is currently experiencing, the joy of God. It doesn't matter that he sits in prison. As we discovered in our study of Philippians 4, Paul is someone who has learned the secret of being content in spite of his surrounding conditions and circumstances. The joy of God holds greater influence over him than any outside forces. Paul possesses this joy. How did he get it?

Faithfulness, Fruitfulness, Fulfillment

We can look back to the Bible passages we've covered over the last three chapters and get the answer to this question, for there's a powerful connection between faithfulness and fruitfulness and the joy of God.

I'm sure you recall the two servants from Jesus' parable of the talents who faithfully invested what the master had entrusted to them. Though they differed in what they initially received and the results they produced, they both heard the same commendation from their master: "Well done, good and faithful servant. You have been faithful over a little; I will set you over much. Enter into the joy of your master." The implication for us is clear: When we faithfully invest what God has entrusted to us, we enter into our Master's joy.

The same thing is true regarding fruit-bearing. In John 15, Jesus spoke at length about fruit-bearing. He reminded us that He's the Vine, His Father is the Vinedresser, and we're the branches. We're to abide in Him, for we can do nothing apart from Him. It's the Father's will that we bear fruit, and to this end He prunes us that we may bear more fruit. Jesus then declared, "My Father is glorified by this, that you bear much fruit, and so prove to be My disciples."

Bringing this teaching to a conclusion, Jesus added this: "These things I have spoken to you *so that My joy may be in you, and that your joy may be made full.*" As a result of bearing fruit, Jesus says, you'll enter into the joy of God. It isn't a result of outward conditions and circumstances; this joy is "in you." It's given to you as the product of fruit-bearing. If you bear fruit—whether the inner kind or the outer kind—you'll experience the joy of God within.

This was the exact experience of the seventy followers of Jesus who Jesus sent out to do ministry, as we read about in Luke 10: "The Lord appointed seventy others, and sent them in pairs ahead of Him to every city and place where He Himself was going to come." After giving them a clear list of instructions, He sent them on their way.

Afterward, "the seventy returned *with joy*" (10:17). Luke's phrasing here is significant. Of all the words he might have used, he chose that word *joy* as the most fitting description of their experience.

Filled with this joy, these disciples reported to Jesus, "Lord, even the demons are subject to us in Your name" (10:17). They'd been able to heal people oppressed by the Devil. This is the fruit of Christlike influence. While Luke doesn't record that Jesus responded with, "Well done, good and faithful servants," He may have indeed spoken those words, as they were certainly true. The seventy had been faithful to carry out Jesus' instructions and do what He would have done in their place. By being faithful and bearing the fruit of Christlike influence, the seventy entered into and experienced the joy of God.

Our experience of joy is connected to both faithfulness and fruitfulness—as taught by Jesus, and as evidenced by the seventy who demonstrated both. Apart from God, this joy is not only explainable, but unattainable, for it is *His* joy.

Knowing the Joy of God

What exactly is the joy of God? Let me take a shot at describing it by explaining and illustrating three phrases.

1. The joy of God is a deeply satisfying sense of fulfillment.

If God has ever worked through you to make an impact on something or someone, you probably know what I'm referring to here. Perhaps you've said, or heard someone else say, "That was such a fulfilling experience for me," or, "That was very satisfying," or, "That really made me feel good." Such words and phrases reflect an attempt to express the feelings of a heart bursting with satisfaction.

This is a feeling that can't be purchased for any price; it's indeed priceless. Do you know what I'm talking about?

You probably *do* know, if God has ever moved through you to lead another person into a relationship with Him; or poured His truth through you, resulting in someone else's freedom from bondage; or dispensed His wisdom and counsel through you, and as a result someone has received much-needed direction; or let you be His vessel of generosity to meet someone else's need; or made you the answer to someone else's prayer; or in any other way empowered you to serve someone and meet a need.

If, on the other hand, you've never felt God move through you to make an impact on His behalf, you've missed out on this satisfying sense of fulfillment. I'm referring to something far deeper and much more meaningful than the good feeling that follows an act of kindness or generosity. Such deeds touch upon what I'm talking about, but in the end fall short of what happens within when God channels His presence, power, and provision through you. This deeply satisfying sense of fulfillment is unexplainable and unattainable apart from God. This is the experience of His joy in you.

2. The joy of God is an affirming sense of personal worth.

We live in a day and age when so many people are struggling to discover personal worth and value. We call it self-esteem. Stop in at a bookstore and ask for a book on self-esteem, and you'll probably be shown shelf after shelf. I did this exact thing out of curiosity some time ago, and was told by the attendant that they carried approximately five hundred titles on the topics of self-esteem and self-improvement. Apparently many people are hungry to feel better about themselves.

In terms of self-esteem, Christians have a distinct advantage: "For we are His workmanship, created in Christ Jesus" (Eph. 2:10). If every Christian truly understood those nine words, they would never lack for

self-esteem. In my book *Experiencing LeaderShift*, I shared the following
illustration to explain the personal significance of that passage:

> MaryAnn and I had been married for only a couple of
> years when she suggested we go to Paris for a short vaca-
> tion. Working as a flight attendant, she'd been there before
> and wanted us to go together. With her travel benefits the
> trip was very affordable.
>
> So off to Paris we went, with plans to take in all the major
> "must experience" places in our few days there. One of them
> was the Louvre. Understand, I'm not an art museum kind of
> guy. Chicago, where I grew up, has a world-class art museum,
> but I've only seen it from the outside. I've never had a desire
> to go in. But this was Paris, and the Louvre is probably the
> most famous art museum in the world. I felt obligated to go.
> Having MaryAnn along slowed me down a bit, but I was still
> able to get in and out in less than an hour. (My apologies to
> those of you who truly appreciate great art.)
>
> Inside the Louvre one of the must-sees is the famous
> painting *Mona Lisa*. As I stood in the back of a rather large
> room, I thought, *Well, there she is!* Guards stood beside the
> painting, and the red ropes prevented us from getting up
> close. Few works of art are valuable enough to receive such
> special treatment. In fact in that very room hung three
> larger paintings (each covered an entire wall), all of which
> I found to be more impressive than *Mona Lisa*. Yet *Mona
> Lisa*, I was told, is considered priceless. "What makes her
> so valuable?" I asked. The answer: "She was painted by

Leonardo da Vinci." The painting itself wasn't so special; the person who created it was special.

Years later, as I sat pondering Ephesians 2:10, the Holy Spirit brought back to mind the day I saw *Mona Lisa*, and I sensed Him saying, "If that painting is priceless—an inanimate object hanging on a wall created by a man who's been dead five hundred years—what does that say for *your* value, as a living work of art created by the living God?"

The fact that "we are His workmanship, created in Christ Jesus," and that we were "purchased with His own blood" (Acts 20:28) makes us more than priceless. It's worth stopping for a moment to contemplate the profound nature of this truth. Here is the source of true self-esteem.

Of course, in communicating to us our value in His eyes, God didn't stop with those first nine words in Ephesians 2:10. The verse goes on to say we were created in Christ Jesus "for good works, which God prepared beforehand so that we should walk in them." Our value is not theoretical. It's not something to simply ponder; it's something for us to *experience*. God, in His grace, gives expression to our worth by creating us *for* something. We don't merely hang on a wall; we walk through life, and as we do, God leads us to good works, which we have the opportunity to carry out.[4]

When God releases His presence, His power, His truth, His wisdom, His generosity, and His goodness through you, He enables you to experience your worth as His workmanship, created in Christ Jesus. Wow! I believe this is a dimension of His joy—unexplainable, and unattainable, apart from God.

3. The joy of God is a passionate sense of calling.

Let me take you back to John 15 where Jesus tells His closest disciples, "You did not choose Me but I chose you, and appointed you that you would go and bear fruit." These young men were called—selected, chosen, handpicked, appointed—to go and bear fruit. The same was true of the seventy in Luke 10: "The Lord *appointed* seventy others, and sent them." They too were called.

This idea of calling isn't uniquely reserved for the Twelve or the seventy, or those who work in vocational ministry. It's a central fact of life for all who call themselves followers of Jesus. Every Christian is called by Jesus to live faithfully and to bear much fruit. It's this calling that brings true meaning and purpose to life. To be engaged in building the kingdom of God is to be engaged in something so much bigger than self. It's to be involved in accomplishing that which will last forever.

Don't you long to be a part of something that's bigger than you, and something that will last forever? It's this sense of calling that gives purpose and meaning to the common activities and mundane responsibilities of life.

This is such an important idea that I'll address it more fully in a later chapter. For now, let me ask you: Do you live with a passionate sense of calling? We live in a day when so many people are just going through the motions, existing day to day, merely trying to keep it all together. Perhaps this explains why those who live with a passionate sense of calling stand out among the crowd of humanity. Such people are unexplainable apart from God.

Why God Wants Us to Know Joy

Why is it so important from God's perspective that we enter into His joy?

There are two simple reasons.

First, He loves us and wants us to be blessed personally by the life that's found in Him. Who of us doesn't want to live with a deeply satisfying sense of fulfillment and an affirming sense of personal worth and a passionate sense of calling? God has placed a desire for each of these in every human heart. Surely, when Jesus said, "I came that they may have life, and have it abundantly" (John 10:10), these phrases are a part of what He has in mind for everyone. God wants to bless you with His joy out of His great love for you.

Second, God wants to display Himself to others through you, and by doing so, *point others to Him*. By enabling you to enter into and experience His joy, as I've sought to describe, God is put on display. This is the ultimate purpose of life. And when it's being achieved, it screams success in the most significant of ways.

So let me ask you these questions, in summary of what we've looked at thus far about unexplainable success:

Are you being *faithful?*

Are you *bearing fruit*—the fruit of Christlike character and the fruit of Christlike influence?

And are you *experiencing the joy of God* as evidenced by …

- a deeply satisfying sense of fulfillment?
- an affirming sense of personal worth?
- a passionate sense of calling?

In the eyes of God, these are the evidences of success.

Discussion Questions

1. Over what experiences in life have you most experienced the joy of God? Explain.

2. What are you involved in doing currently that enables you to experience a deeply satisfying sense of fulfillment and an affirming sense of personal worth?

3. Is there anything for which you feel a passionate sense of calling? Explain.

4. Do you sense God calling you and leading you to do anything at the present time that would enable you to more deeply experience His joy?

13

THE ULTIMATE MEASURE OF SUCCESS

Whether, then, you eat or drink or whatever
you do, do all to the glory of God.

1 CORINTHIANS 10:31

The popular use of the phrase "the bottom line" as something more than a technical accounting term traces back only to the 1960s. It's hard to believe it wasn't used more widely before then, since it's now so much a part of our everyday vocabulary. We use it to mean "the final result or statement; the upshot; the main or essential point." When we tell someone, "Just give me the bottom line," that person knows exactly what's being requested, whether or not it involves finances.

In this chapter, I want to give you the bottom line on success. This is it: *Make God famous.*

Paul puts it this way: "Whether, then, you eat or drink or whatever you do, *do all to the glory of God*" (1 Cor. 10:31). He reminds us, "For from Him and through Him and to Him are all things. *To Him be the glory forever. Amen"* (Rom. 11:36).

God Himself describes His people as those who are "called by My name, and whom I have created *for My glory"* (Isa. 43:7).

The framers of the Westminster Shorter Catechism expressed it this way: "The chief end of man is *to glorify God* and enjoy Him forever."

Rick Warren said it well in these opening lines from his best-selling book *The Purpose-Driven Life*:

> It's not about you. The purpose of your life is far greater than your own personal fulfillment, your peace of mind, or even your happiness. It's far greater than your family, your career, or even your wildest dreams and ambitions. If you want to know why you were placed on this planet, you must begin with God. You were born *by* his purpose and *for* his purpose.[5]

This purpose—*your* purpose—is to bring glory to God's name … to make Him famous. You were created by God, for God. This is the bottom line on success, and the bottom line on life itself.

We're called to be faithful in order to bring a return for the Master. We're called and appointed to bear fruit to bring glory to the Father. Jesus said, *"My Father is glorified by this,* that you bear much fruit, and so prove to be My disciples." As for the experience of His joy, John Piper puts it well when he says, "God is most glorified with us when we are most satisfied in Him."

Our faithfulness, our fruitfulness, and our fulfillment are all intended to make Him famous. This is the ultimate measure of success in life.

So how do we do it? How can we live to make God famous? What can we do to bring Him glory?

Below are four responses to these questions, each of them equally important.

Putting His Attributes on Display

David begins Psalm 19 this way: "The heavens are telling the glory of God; and their expanse is declaring the work of His hands." Just look up, David is saying, and you can see God on display. His power and majesty and brilliance are clear to see. This is what creation reveals.

In Revelation 4:11, we read, "Worthy are You, our Lord and our God, to receive glory and honor and power; for *You created all things, and because of your will they exsisted, and were created."* Take a look around, for the evidence for God is all around you.

Jesus Himself was sent to earth to reveal the attributes of God, as we learn in John's gospel: "The Word became flesh and dwelt among us, and we saw His glory, glory as of the only begotten from the Father, full of grace and truth" (John 1:14).

As God's creation, you and I are called to put His attributes on display. How do we do that?

Several years ago, a friend called, asking if I would be willing to help him and his wife put a structure in place for their newly formed charitable foundation. I was honored to help them, so a few days later I met with them at their home to begin the process.

Early in our conversation, I asked them, "Why do you want to start a foundation?" It was a basic question, and I assumed I knew the answer—so they could give financially to causes that proclaimed the name of Jesus. I was only asking because I wanted to hear *them* say it, in their own words.

My friend surprised me by saying, "We want to put the generosity of God on display."

I asked for further explanation.

"In the short time we've been Christians," he said, "we've found that most people, Christians included, think God is stingy. This has certainly not been our experience and we want to do what we can to change that perception of God. We want to display His generosity."

That approach had a fundamental effect on the shaping of the foundation. For example, they didn't name the foundation after themselves. Instead, a biblical name was chosen, reflecting the generosity of God. I found this seemingly simple act to be a profound one that said, "This foundation is based on God's generosity, not ours."

This is a good illustration of how all of life should be. The way we relate to people should display the nature and attributes of God.

This is exactly what Jesus said to His disciples in the upper room on the night before His crucifixion: "By this all men will know that you are My disciples, if you have love for one another" (John 13:35). Treating people with love puts the love of God on display.

In the same way, God should be on display in us as we work—and, in fact, in all our involvements. Remember again Paul's words in Colossians 3:23: *"Whatever you do,"* he instructs us, "do your work heartily, as for the Lord rather than for men." God's own passion and excellence should be reflected in how we do all that we do. Our participation in the marketplace should be marked by integrity, honesty, and quality, both in our product as well as in the sales and service of that product.

We also have a major opportunity to display the attributes of God in how we face and walk through trials. In such times, the strength, the power, the kindness, the mercy, the grace of God become evident through us. This is exactly what Paul states in the midst of discussing a particularly severe trial of his own in 2 Corinthians 12:7–10: "Most gladly therefore, I will rather boast about my weaknesses," he writes, "so that the power of Christ may dwell in me."

Life itself is to be a platform from which the nature and the attributes of God are put on display. As Jesus said,

> You are the light of the world. A city set on a hill cannot
> be hidden. Nor does anyone light a lamp and put it under
> a basket, but on a lampstand, and it gives light to all who
> are in the house. Let your light shine before men in such a
> way that they may see your good works, and glorify your
> Father who is in heaven. (Matt. 5:14–16)

So what are people discovering about God, based on knowing and watching you?

We have the opportunity to make Him famous by living in a way that puts on display His love, His generosity, His kindness, His mercy, His excellence, His peace, and so much more. As God's workmanship, created in Christ Jesus for good works, you're like God's painting or sculpture on display to make Him famous.

Assigning Him Credit

We make God famous when we give Him the credit He deserves. David encourages this when he writes in Psalm 29:1, "Ascribe to the LORD, O sons of the mighty, ascribe to the LORD glory and strength." He does the same in the song of thanksgiving he establishes in 1 Chronicles 16: "Sing to the LORD, all the earth; proclaim good tidings of His salvation from day to day. Tell of His glory among the nations, His wonderful deeds among all the peoples" (16:23–24).

One of my favorite stories reflecting this truth is found in Acts 3. Peter and John, on their way to the temple, encountered a man who'd been crippled since birth. Unable to work to support himself, he was reduced to begging. Peter said to him, "I do not possess silver and gold, but what I do have I give to you: In the name of Jesus Christ the Nazarene—walk" (3:6).

After Peter lifted him up, this man "stood upright and began to walk" (3:8). As you would expect, the surrounding crowd was astonished and came running to Peter and John. Peter responded,

Men of Israel, why are you amazed at this, or why do
you gaze at us, as if by our own power or piety we had
made him walk? The God of Abraham, Isaac and Jacob,
the God of our fathers, has glorified His servant Jesus....
On the basis of faith in His name, it is the name of Jesus
which has strengthened this man whom you see and know.
(3:12–16)

How tempting it is for us to take credit for what we do and accomplish.

I mentioned earlier my friends who started a foundation. They decided to include a cover letter with each and every check that came from the foundation, and because of their desire to proclaim God's generosity, this cover letter quoted Deuteronomy 8:18: "You shall remember the LORD your God, for it is He who is giving you the power to make wealth." They wanted recipients of the foundation's gifts to know that God was behind this check from the very beginning—for He alone grants us the ability to produce wealth.

I recently had lunch with three businessmen who wanted to discuss how they could more intentionally and effectively honor God through their business. They wanted to "invest" what they'd been given by God in a way that paid dividends for eternity. They were prospering in the midst of difficult economic times, and they were absolutely convinced that God was the source of their prosperity. They explained how unexpected clients came from unexpected places and unsolicited sources. They said there was no explanation for this, apart from God's intervention. In addition, some new projects involving new technology had emerged, for which they simply shook their heads and said, "It's been God."

I've found that when people truly believe that God is the source of their supply, their articulation of that fact is received as genuine and sincere. We can make God famous by giving Him the credit for that which is accomplished.

We can also assign God the credit for strengthening us in the midst of trial. As my friend Cindy talked on that airplane with Sam and Mary, she made it clear that God had sustained her and Dave following the death of their son. God was their source of strength and hope.

If you find it difficult to sincerely give God credit, it's probably because you don't truly see Him as deserving such recognition. If this is the case, you're believing a lie—for He alone is the giver of every good gift (James 1:17).

As David wrote, "Ascribe to the LORD glory and strength" (Ps. 29:1). When we do that, we help make God famous.

Pointing Others to Him

We live in a day when we tend to "glorify" great messengers rather than the greatness of their message and the One from whom their message originated. But Peter tells us,

> Whoever speaks, is to do so as one who is speaking the utterances of God; whoever serves is to do so as one who is serving by the strength which God supplies; so that in all things God may be glorified through Jesus Christ, to whom belongs the glory and dominion forever and ever. Amen. (1 Peter 4:11)

The "speaking" that Peter refers to here is the teaching of God's truth. Those who teach should do so in a way that points to God. It should be clear that this is *His* truth.

The same should be true of those who serve. I remember years ago when one particular "television evangelist" offered to mail a piece of paper showing his handprint to any who were in need of physical healing. He said that if those who were sick or injured simply placed his handprint on their infirmity, there was a good chance they would be healed.

While most of us laugh and scoff at such an offer, and deservedly so, how few of us actually look to God for healing.

I attended a conference recently in which one particular speaker asked their audience how many of them ever heard their fathers pray for God's healing when they were sick or injured as a child. Out of an audience of well over a hundred, only three raised their hands.

If we want to point our children to God, we should turn toward God with our children whenever and wherever possible. If we want to proclaim to them that God is the Great Physician, we should be asking God for their healing when the need arises. While God uses medical science, and we should access all that God provides, we cannot afford to underestimate His desire and power to heal. When we point others to God, we help increase His fame in their eyes.

Following Him into the Realm of the Unexplainable

How many times have you heard it said of someone, "He's a self-made man"? While this is intended as a compliment, it's actually one of the last things any Christian should want said of them. It should rather be, "He's a God-made man," or, "She's a God-made woman." If who you are, what you do, how you do it, how you got to where you are, and what you've accomplished is explainable in human terms, your life merely points to you.

Our lives on many levels should be unexplainable apart from God. If this isn't the case, then at the risk of sounding harsh, let me say that you've failed to follow God's leading. God is beyond us. As He Himself said, "My thoughts are not your thoughts, nor are your ways My ways, declares the LORD" (Isa. 55:8). God created you to point to Him, and one of the clearest ways He does this is by making you—and the unfolding of your life—unexplainable apart from Him.

"We walk by faith, not by sight" (2 Cor. 5:7). Walking by faith means we're to live in dependence upon God. When we do walk by faith, God proves Himself faithful, and His greatness is put on display.

Are you in a place of dependence upon Him? Let me ask it this way: What would change in your life if God were *not* leading you? If your answer is, "not much," it simply means God is not leading you.

Let me ask it another way: If the Holy Spirit were removed from your life, what would be different? Again, if your honest answer is "nothing, really," it means you're not walking in the Spirit.

The facts seem to indicate that many who claim to be Christians are living "by sight," in the realm of the explainable. The divorce rate among Christians is virtually the same as it is among non-Christians. The lifestyle of many Christians appears to reflect an enjoyment perspective rather than an investment perspective toward life.

God dwells in the realm of the unexplainable. He did the unexplainable when He sent His Son to earth in the form of a man to dwell among us, and ultimately to give His life for us. He now calls us to follow Him into the realm of the unexplainable so that our lives point to Him. This is the purpose for which we were created—to make Him famous. To succeed in life, as God defines success, is to fulfill that purpose.

So how are you doing? How does your bottom line look? In what ways are His attributes being displayed in and through you? How can you give Him credit for what's taking place in your life? In what ways are you pointing others to Him? What is occurring in, through, and around your life for which there's no explanation apart from God?

To make Him famous—this is life's bottom line.

Discussion Questions

1. In what ways can you put the attributes of God on display to the world around you? Be specific.

2. What has occurred in your life recently for which you can and should give God credit?

3. In what specific ways can you play a role in pointing someone to God? Explain and be as specific as possible.

4. What would change in your life right now if God were not actively leading you? If the Holy Spirit were taken out of your life, what would be different?

5. What will be your personal "takeaways" from these chapters (11, 12, and 13)?

PART THREE

UNEXPLAINABLE SIGNIFICANCE

Lifeshift 3: From Mine to His

14

DISCOVERING SIGNIFICANCE

For we are His workmanship, created in Christ
Jesus for good works, which God prepared
beforehand so that we would walk in them.

EPHESIANS 2:10

You are significant!

Don't believe me? Listen to the following words, for they provide the basis for that statement and claim:

> Then God said, "Let Us make man in Our image, accord-
> ing to Our likeness...." God created man in His own
> image, in the image of God He created him; male and
> female He created them. (Gen. 1:26–27)

Significance is defined as the quality of being important. Whether we're talking about an object, an idea, or a person, to be significant is to have worth, value, and importance.

Of course the opposite of significance is to be lacking value, worth, and importance. I'm hard-pressed to think of a more cruel thing to say or hear than the words, "You're worthless," or, "You're a no-account." Contrary to the childhood rhyme about the harmless effect of name-calling, these words hurt and will leave a scar on anyone who receives them. Such words strike at the very heart of one's value as a person. And they're always wrong—a lie.

God created you in His image—you can't get any more significant than that.

Because you bear the label "made by God," your significance is derived from Him—the most significant entity in all the universe. Therefore, you have a God-given desire to feel significant, in keeping with who you are.

Where Significance Is Found

Man's desire to be significant can be seen as far back as the garden of Eden. In fact, this desire played a pivotal role in man's fall, as we see when we review the story:

> Now the serpent was more crafty than any beast of the field which the LORD God had made. And he said to the woman, "Indeed, has God said, 'You shall not eat from any tree of the garden'?"
>
> The woman said to the serpent, "From the fruit of the trees of the garden we may eat; but from the fruit of the tree which is in the middle of the garden, God has said, 'You shall not eat from it or touch it, or you will die.'"
>
> The serpent said to the woman, "You surely will not die! For God knows that in the day you eat from it your eyes

will be opened, and you will be like God, knowing good
and evil."

When the woman saw that the tree was good for food,
and that it was a delight to the eyes, and that the tree was
desirable to make one wise, she took from its fruit and
ate; and she gave also to her husband with her, and he ate.
(Gen. 3:1–6)

Satan began by calling into question the truth of God's Word: "Has
God said …?" Following Eve's response, he moved from question to statement: "You surely will not die." In other words, *God lied to you.*

Satan went on to say, "For God knows that in the day you eat from
it your eyes will be opened, and you will be like God, knowing good and
evil." You—*you,* Eve—can be like God. You can *know* more than you know,
you can *be* more than you are—in fact, you can *be like God Himself.* But
God doesn't want this to happen, so He lied to you about the consequences
of eating that forbidden fruit.

As Eve considered this, she decided to eat of the forbidden fruit, and
convinced Adam to do the same. It wasn't merely the appeal of the fruit
as food that caused their fall; it was the appeal of being more significant.
They believed Satan's lie that they could experience a greater measure of
importance. Being created by God was good, but not as good as being like
God Himself.

Satan knew the power of this temptation. It was this same temptation,
based on the exact same desire for significance, that caused his own fall
sometime earlier. That story is told in Isaiah 14:

How you have fallen from heaven,
O star of the morning, son of the dawn!

You have been cut down to the earth,

You who have weakened the nations!

But you said in your heart,

"I will ascend to heaven;

I will raise my throne above the stars of God,

And I will sit on the mount of assembly

In the recesses of the north.

I will ascend above the heights of the clouds;

I will make myself like the Most High."

(Isa. 14:12–14)

Did you note the pattern?

I will ascend …

I will raise …

I will sit …

I will ascend …

I will make myself …

Satan himself wanted to be more significant than he was. He too had wanted to be like God. He mistakenly believed there was a way to be more significant than he already was.

In both cases, *self* became the focus. This beautiful angel whom God had created and given a place of great authority (as we see in Ezekiel 28) shifted his focus from God to himself: *I will … I will … I will … I will … I will …* In the same way, Adam and Eve took their eyes off of God and looked at themselves.

For each of them, self-interest and self-promotion became the focus, and this shift led to their falls.

For Adam and Eve, their choice to act out of self-interest and self-promotion led not to feelings of greater significance, but to feelings of great shame. Their sense of true significance was lost.

True significance comes from God. We derive ours from His. Only by focusing on His interests and living to promote Him do we experience and feel our own significance—our true worth, value, and importance.

Satan of course sings the same tune to us today that he did to Eve in the garden of Eden. He's still trying to get each of us to buy into the idea that we can satisfy our longing for significance by satisfying our own interests and promoting our own image. But this will yield only a false or counterfeit significance—a poor substitute for the real thing. That which Satan offers is achieved by becoming significant in the eyes of the world, which can never measure up to significance in the eyes of God.

Plenty of Warning

As we evaluate our search for significance, it's good to remember this warning Jesus issued about self-glory:

> Beware of practicing your righteousness before men to be
> noticed by them; otherwise you have no reward with your
> Father who is in heaven. (Matt. 6:1)

After this verse, Jesus went on to address giving, praying, and fasting, warning us that there's a temptation to do these things not for God's glory but for our own. He says that if we do these things for self-glory, self-glory will be our only reward.

In Acts 5, we read of a story that reveals the true danger of this very thing:

> But a man named Ananias, with his wife Sapphira, sold
> a piece of property, and kept back some of the price for
> himself, with his wife's full knowledge, and bringing a
> portion of it, he laid it at the apostles' feet.

But Peter said, "Ananias, why has Satan filled your heart to lie to the Holy Spirit and to keep back some of the price of the land? While it remained unsold, did it not remain your own? And after it was sold, was it not under your control? Why is it that you have conceived this deed in your heart? You have not lied to men but to God."

And as he heard these words, Ananias fell down and breathed his last; and great fear came over all who heard of it. (Acts 5:1–5)

Why would Ananias and his wife, Sapphira, do such a thing? No one was forcing them to sell their property. No one was twisting their arm to make this contribution. What was their motivation for doing so and then lying about it?

This is the exact question that Peter asks Ananias, and later Sapphira. Unfortunately, we never hear their answers. We're left to figure out the answer for ourselves from the context of the story.

In order to understand the context, we need to look back at what happened just before they sold their property. Immediately before this passage, Luke describes how the first Christians served and helped each other:

For there was not a needy person among them, for all who were owners of land or houses would sell them and bring the proceeds of the sales and lay them at the apostles' feet, and they would be distributed to each as any had need. Now Joseph, a Levite of Cyprian birth, who was also called Barnabas by the apostles (which translated means

Son of Encouragement), and who owned a tract of land, sold it and brought the money and laid it at the apostles' feet. (Acts 4:34–37)

We can put two and two together and assume that Barnabas had received quite a bit of "press" inside and outside the church as a result of his generosity. He may well have been recognized as a man of great importance in the eyes of others. Ananias and Sapphira, it appears, wanted to experience the same recognition, so they decided to sell their property and do as Barnabas did with the proceeds.

There was just one difference: While Barnabas was motivated by God's interests and glory, Ananias and Sapphira were motivated by self-interest and personal glory. Because they believed a lie, they later ended up telling a lie. They had bought into Satan's deception that they could satisfy their longing for significance by becoming important in the eyes of others. It ended up costing them their lives—literally.

Satan works hard to convince us that the only way to feel our true worth is through self-promotion in the eyes of the world. He tells us that this can be done through four As—*achieve, accomplish, attain,* and *accumulate.* The world highly esteems those who achieve great heights and accomplish great tasks. The world recognizes as important those who attain prominence and accumulate the world's goods. We naturally conclude that we'll be seen as valuable and recognized as important if we gain what the world esteems and recognizes as important. This is what Satan wants us to believe, for such pursuits shift our focus from God to self.

A Great Man's Reflections

This is exactly what happened to Solomon, who started out so strongly but later went astray. Solomon reflected on this as he neared the end of his life:

I enlarged my works: I built houses for myself, I planted vineyards for myself; I made gardens and parks for myself and I planted in them all kinds of fruit trees; I made ponds of water for myself from which to irrigate a forest of growing trees. I bought male and female slaves and I had homeborn slaves. Also I possessed flocks and herds larger than all who preceded me in Jerusalem. Also, I collected for myself silver and gold and the treasure of kings and provinces. I provided for myself male and female singers and the pleasures of men—many concubines. Then I became great and increased more than all who preceded me in Jerusalem. My wisdom also stood by me. And all that my eyes desired I did not refuse them. I did not withhold my heart from any pleasure, for my heart was pleased because of all my labor and this was my reward for all my labor. (Eccl. 2:4–10)

The fact that Solomon "became great and increased more than all who preceded" him in Jerusalem was evidenced by his ability to satisfy every desire of his eye and every pleasure of his heart.

In the next verse, he sums up the true value of all these pursuits:

Thus I considered all my activities which my hands had done and the labor which I had exerted, *and behold all was vanity and striving after wind and there was no profit under the sun.* (2:11)

He soon explains his thoughts further:

Then I said to myself, "As is the fate of the fool, it will also befall me. Why then have I been extremely wise?"

> So I said to myself, "This too is vanity." For there is no
> lasting remembrance of the wise man as with the fool,
> inasmuch as in the coming days all will be forgotten.
> And how the wise man and the fool alike die! So I hated
> life, for the work which had been done under the sun
> was grievous to me; because everything is futility and
> striving after wind.
>
> Thus I hated all the fruit of my labor for which I had
> labored under the sun, for I must leave it to the man who
> will come after me. And who knows whether he will be a
> wise man or a fool? Yet he will have control over all the
> fruit of my labor for which I have labored by acting wisely
> under the sun. This too is vanity. Therefore I completely
> despaired of all the fruit of my labor for which I had
> labored under the sun. (2:15–20)

He then draws a bottom-line conclusion:

> There is nothing better for a man than to eat and drink
> and tell himself that his labor is good. This also I have seen
> that it is from the hand of God. For who can eat and who
> can have enjoyment without Him? (2:24–25)

This wise old man eventually realized that his focus on self—"vanity," as he calls it—was equivalent to chasing the wind. He came to know that everything truly valuable is derived from God. Everything, he now understands, is *from* God and *for* God.

Therefore, his counsel to us is to focus on God: "To the degree that you achieve," he would say, "achieve for God's glory. To the degree that you accomplish anything, accomplish for the sake of God's kingdom. To the degree that you attain and accumulate what the world has to offer, do it for the purposes of God. In God you'll find your significance."

Jesus put it this way: "For whoever wishes to save his life will lose it; but whoever loses his life for My sake will find it" (Matt. 16:25). Life is found when we give our lives to Jesus.

Jesus also expressed it this way: "It is more blessed to give than to receive" (Acts 20:35). We don't experience our worth by getting what the world recognizes. We experience it as we give ourselves away for the glory of God. His message is so radical! He said the humble will be exalted; He said those who want to be great should be the servant; He said those who desire to be first will end up being last. In all this, Jesus is saying that we'll never find fullness of life by pursuing self-interest; we'll find ourselves only as we pursue God. Our significance is found in Him, for we were created in His image.

Paul's Lifeshift

I'm writing of a needed lifeshift—from a focus on me to a focus on Him; from trying to make myself significant in the eyes of the world to making Him significant in the eyes of the world.

This lifeshift is one that Paul himself made:

> Although I myself might have confidence even in the flesh. If anyone else has a mind to put confidence in the flesh, I far more: circumcised the eighth day, of the nation of Israel, of the tribe of Benjamin, a Hebrew of Hebrews; as to the Law, a Pharisee; as to zeal, a persecutor of the church; as to the righteousness which is in the Law, found blameless. (Phil. 3:4–6)

Paul's credentials had made him a person of great importance in the world around him. Here's how he eventually evaluated those credentials:

> But whatever things were gain to me, those things I have counted as loss for the sake of Christ. More than that, I count all things to be loss in view of the surpassing value of knowing Christ Jesus my Lord, for whom I have suffered the loss of all things, and count them but rubbish so that I may gain Christ. (3:7–8)

As a result of this shift in thinking, Paul had a new focus:

> I press on toward the goal for the prize of the upward call of God in Christ Jesus. (v. 14)

Now advanced in years, Paul looks back in reflection on life, just as Solomon had done. But look how different Paul's reflections are:

> I have fought the good fight, I have finished the course, I have kept the faith; in the future there is laid up for me the crown of righteousness, which the Lord, the righteous Judge, will award to me on that day; and not only to me, but also to all who have loved His appearing. (2 Tim. 4:7–8)

Here's a man who feels his significance. He looks forward to receiving the crown of righteousness, which he clearly believes is awaiting him.

And the good news for you and me? We can receive the same crown. The ultimate expression of our significance will be experienced when we enter into God's very presence and become partakers of His glory … forever.

Start Now

The time to start the journey there is now. Since your significance is found in God—for you were created in His image—allow no further delay in seeking after His interests. Promote His name in all the earth. Then you'll know true significance within.

In the next five chapters, we'll look specifically at what it means to shift the focus of our significance from "mine" to "His."

Discussion Questions

1. What were you raised to believe about the source of personal significance?

2. How has that understanding shaped your life?

3. To what degree has your own sense of significance been built upon the four As—*achieve, accomplish, attain, accumulate*? (1 = *not at all*, 10 = *almost totally*.)

4. What would "achieving" for God's glory look like for you? Describe it as specifically and practically as possible.

5. To what degree do you feel significant in the eyes of God? (Use a one-to-ten scale: 1 = *I feel like a no-count to God;* 10 = *I feel treasured and highly valued by God.*)

15

FOLLOWING GOD'S CALL

*Therefore I, the prisoner of the Lord, implore
you to walk in a manner worthy of the calling
with which you have been called.*

EPHESIANS 4:1

"I don't ever want you to simply get a job," I told my two college-age sons one day.

"I know this sounds contrary to everything you've heard from the world around you," I continued. "I know our culture preaches, 'Get a good education, so you can get a good job.' The world defines a good job as one that provides good money. Well, as your father, I want to encourage you to do something with your life that flows from your calling." I made it clear to them that providing financially for their needs was a reality and a God-ordained responsibility—but one that's secondary in importance to our responsibility to follow our calling.

I also have a daughter who's currently a senior in high school, and in the coming months I'll be having this same conversation with her.

You may be thinking that I want my children to pursue some sort of vocational ministry work—each becoming a pastor or missionary, or perhaps a teacher, social worker, or something similar. Well, I can assure you that's not the case.

I believe many people hold a mistaken view of calling. Most seem to believe that pastors and missionaries and others who have chosen to forsake personal gain in order to serve others have done so because they were somehow "called" to do so. In contrast, the remaining members of society simply pursue work as a means of making money.

The language we use often reflects this perspective. Professional ministry people, for example, are often asked to explain their "call." In contrast, it's not very often that we hear our mechanic or our insurance agent refer to being "called" to their work. The average marketplace job seems to fall under some other heading than "calling." Without a sense of calling, the significance of one's work is greatly reduced and the primary purpose does indeed become making money.

As I talked with my boys, I went on to explain that this is an inaccurate understanding of "calling." There's just no biblical basis to believe that God "calls" some people to a role of great significance while relegating the remaining majority to simply "work" for the purpose of making money.

What's Our Calling?

Whether you think of yourself as having a job or having a calling has virtually nothing to do with what you actually "do for a living." On the other hand, it has everything to do with your perspective toward what you do.

Possessing the right perspective flows from an accurate understanding of this concept of God's call—so let's start there.

In Ephesians 4:1, Paul writes, "Therefore I, the prisoner of the Lord, implore you to walk in a manner worthy of the *calling* with which you have been *called.*" Who is Paul speaking to here? This is an important question, because it reveals just who it is that has such a calling.

If we look back to the opening verse of the Ephesian letter, Paul says he's addressing "the saints who are at Ephesus and who are faithful in Christ Jesus." Paul is writing to all the followers of Jesus in the city of Ephesus. So when he later speaks to them of "a calling," he's not referring to some select group of people, but rather to all "who are faithful in Christ Jesus." All of us who fit within that description have the same calling—and this calling is to a relationship with Jesus.

If you've ever studied Paul's letter to the Ephesians, you know that its first three chapters are devoted to explaining what it means to be in relationship with Jesus. In fact, within the first thirteen verses, the phrase *in Christ* appears in some form eleven different times. God's calling us to a relationship with Himself.

As the fourth chapter of this letter opens, Paul makes a shift in focus and begins to explain the implications and applications for everyday life that flow from being in relationship with Jesus, as he challenges us to "walk in a manner worthy of the calling with which you have been called."

That's why you and I need to understand that God's calling is to a relationship, not to a particular form of work. From our relationship with Him, all of life flows and becomes an expression of His influence upon us. Your relationship with Jesus should permeate every arena of your life. As a member of the body of Christ, you're called to participate in certain ways that reflect the presence of Jesus within you.

Paul spells out what this participation in the body looks like throughout the second half of his letter to the Ephesians. We're called to speak and relate to others, and to make moral and behavioral choices, in ways that reflect the presence of Jesus. Likewise Paul says husbands and wives are called to relate to one another in a way that reflects Christ's presence. The same goes for the parent-child relationship: A child is called to treat his or her parents with unconditional respect and honor, and parents are called to raise their children in a way that causes them to want to have their own relationship with Jesus.

Paul then goes on to relate this Christ-centered approach to our work:

> Slaves, be obedient to those who are your masters according to the flesh, with fear and trembling, in the sincerity of your heart, as to Christ; not by way of eyeservice, as men-pleasers, but as slaves of Christ, doing the will of God from the heart. With good will render service, as to the Lord, and not to men, knowing that whatever good thing each one does, this he will receive back from the Lord, whether slave or free. And masters, do the same things to them, and give up threatening, knowing that both their Master and yours is in heaven, and there is no partiality with Him. (Eph. 6:5–9)

God's calling is to a relationship with Himself. Our participation in every arena of life should reflect this relationship. This makes all of life a calling.

Work as a Calling

Have you ever stopped to consider the "work" involvements of the major characters of the Bible?

Abraham was a rancher—and in the world's terms, a very successful one. He was "was very rich in livestock, in silver and in gold" (Gen. 13:2). God had "greatly blessed" him in his ranching business and given Abraham "flocks and herds, and silver and gold, and servants and maids, and camels and donkeys" (Gen. 24:35).

Joseph's first job in Egypt was that of a servant in the house of a government official named Potiphar. Joseph's title: "slave." Following his release from prison after several years there, he began to climb the government ladder and eventually ascended to the second-highest position in all of Egypt, subject only to the pharaoh himself.

Moses spent the first forty years of his life working within the household of Pharaoh. He spent the next forty working for his father-in-law as a shepherd. While he's best known for the leadership he provided to God's people through forty years in the wilderness, God's call upon his life didn't begin at the burning bush. God's call (a relationship with Himself) was upon Moses' life dating back to when his mother placed him in a basket and sent him floating downstream in the Nile River.

David spent his early years working as a shepherd. From there, he assumed a position in King Saul's court. He spent time as a soldier in the army before eventually becoming king himself.

Daniel, of lion's den fame, started out as a teenager serving in King Nebuchadnezzar's court. He too rose within government ranks until he was eventually positioned as one of only three commissioners "in charge of the whole kingdom" (Dan. 6:1–2).

We view each of these men as having a "calling" from God, which they did. Yet not one of them was employed in a situation that fits our common understanding of calling. It's worth noting in particular just how many of them spent significant seasons of their working life engaged as slaves.

In each of their cases, we see that God's influence through them wasn't dependent primarily upon a position they held or a job they performed, but rather upon their relationship with Him. It wasn't what they did that characterized their calling; it was who they did it for. Each of them was led by God to the position they held and the work they performed.

Paul says in Ephesians 6:5–9 that this should be true of us. Slaves were to obey their masters from the heart, as they would Christ Himself; they weren't to work as men-pleasers, but as slaves of Christ; they were to render service as to the Lord and not merely to men, knowing that in the end their ultimate compensation would come from God Himself. And those who "worked" as masters of slaves needed to know that the same truths applied to them.

It's not *what* you do, Paul was emphasizing; it's *who you do it for.* You've been called to a relationship with Jesus, and you need to carry out your work, whatever it may be, in a manner befitting His presence in your life. Seeing Jesus as your boss makes a big difference.

Consider Paul himself at the time he wrote these words. He's a prison inmate. But notice who he believes imprisons him: "Therefore I, the *prisoner of the Lord"* (Eph. 4:1). Paul saw himself not as a prisoner of Rome, but of the Lord. "I'm here by God's doing," he was saying; "this is where God has me." Based on his calling (a relationship with Jesus), he needed to be the kind of inmate who gives evidence to the presence of Jesus in his life.

This is what it means to walk in a manner worthy of your calling.

When we approach our work, whatever it may be, in a way that reflects our calling, the results in and through us will in some ways be unexplainable apart from God. Certainly, the slave who conducted himself according to Paul's instructions would have set himself apart from other slaves. In the same way, masters who saw Jesus as their boss and followed Paul's instructions would have treated their slaves differently. And both slave and master could explain the difference this way: "I have a relationship with Jesus and He influences me to live and work as I do."

We'll further explore this difference—which makes us unexplainable apart from God—in the next chapter. For now, it's critically important for you to know that God has a calling upon your life. And this calling is to live in relationship with Him in every arena of life—including, of course, your place of work.

A Sense of Calling Is Life-Changing

I talk about God's calling with my children because they need to understand that God does indeed have a calling for them, and it's to have a relationship with Him. This is a life-changing perspective of calling for two reasons.

First, as I've been stating, it will deeply impact how they carry out their work, whatever that may be. As it stands right now for my sons, their "work" is summarized in the phrase *student-athlete*. One plays baseball and the other football, and both are full-time students. These two involvements are their current "work." They need to approach being student-athletes as though Jesus were their head coach and their professor in every class, as they strive to "walk in a manner worthy of their calling to which they have been called."

Second, it's from their relationship with God that they'll receive the needed direction pertaining to their future "work." We're instructed in Proverbs 3:5–6, "Trust in the LORD with all your heart and do not lean on your own understanding. In all your ways acknowledge Him, and He will make your paths straight." My three children want to know what God has in store for them in the days to come. Is there a specific "work" that fits who He made them to be, that would enable them to have an impact on others in the name of Jesus, as well as provide a means of financial support? I believe there is—and they believe it too.

Both of my sons are in a season of life where such decisions are right before them. How will they know how to proceed?

They'll need to follow the leading of God, which will flow from their relationship with Him. "For all who are being led by the Spirit of God, these are sons of God" (Rom. 8:14). Will they need a job in the future? Of course they will. But this job, whatever it is, needs to flow from their true calling, which is to live in relationship with Jesus.

Over the course of a lifetime, they may have several different jobs. However, their calling will always remain the same—to follow Jesus and let their lives flow from their relationship with Him. Then when they're asked, "How did you get here, doing what you're doing?" the explanation will be,

"God led me here." And if they do their work as unto the Lord, their efforts and the results achieved will prove to be unexplainable apart from Him.

What about you? Have you responded to God's call to live your life in relationship with Him? If so, how is that call impacting the way you carry out your work, whatever it may be? God wants your efforts, and the results that come from them, to be unexplainable apart from Him. In this way your work can point to God.

And when it does, you'll know true significance—not as the world gives, but as only God can produce within. This is the significance He has designed you for.

Discussion Questions

1. How would you explain God's calling to someone?
2. Do you live with a sense of God's calling? Answer *not at all, somewhat,* or *very much so,* and explain your answer.
3. Do you see your "work" as a calling? Why or why not?
4. What, if anything, would need to change in order for you to more clearly see your work as a calling? Be specific and practical.

16

IS YOUR WORK A CALLING?

Whatever you do, do your work heartily, as for the
Lord rather than for men, knowing that from the
Lord you will receive the reward of the inheritance.
It is the Lord Christ whom you serve.

COLOSSIANS 3:23–24

Because I am "handyman challenged," on several occasions I've solicited the help of a man named Bob to help me with some house projects. While he's officially retired, he enjoys using his "handyman competence" to help poor souls like me. He ends up putting a few bucks in his pocket, and I get a job well done at a very reasonable cost.

When he first started to help out, he called me Pastor Cousins.

Quickly and respectfully, I told him, "My name is Don."

"Okay, Pastor Don," he replied.

"Don will do," I said.

He argued that I'd earned that title and therefore deserved to be called by it.

I countered that if he insisted on the title thing, I would address him as "Builder Bob."

He chuckled and decided that just Don and Bob would be fine.

Titles and labels have become so much a part of our vocabulary—white collar or blue collar, management or labor, salaried or hourly, employer or employee, clergy or laity, and many more. Such labels are ingrained in our cultural language, but it puzzles me why we hang on to them, since they do far more to divide us than to unite us. Business leaders want to build teams, yet utilize titles and labels that undermine the very nature and sense of team. Pastors want their people to see themselves as members of one body, yet reinforce the differences between professional and laity.

Perhaps one reason we hold on to such labels is that they speak to our significance. White collar trumps blue collar, as does management over labor. It's more prestigious to be on salary than it is to punch a clock. You've probably heard people say, "I'm just a janitor," "I'm just a salesclerk," or, "I'm just an assembly line worker." But when was the last time you heard, "I'm just a brain surgeon," or "just a partner in a law firm," or "just the CEO"?

In society, significance is tied to role: Where do you fit? Just how important are you?

The Role and Label We All Share

Thankfully, this isn't how God sees us. In His eyes, our value isn't determined by what we do, or measured by the role we play or the category we fall into. As it relates to our role in life, whatever that may be, the New Testament would use just one label for all of us: *steward.* We're all stewards—managers of that which God has entrusted to us.

John Beckett, in his book *Loving Monday,* writes this:

> Jesus taught extensively concerning stewardship, using
> parables set in the business context of his day. In one,

recorded by Luke, a nobleman entrusted significant wealth to his servants while he went to a distant country. "Do business until I come," he said. He expected them to produce a return on the amounts they had been given. When he came back, he rewarded those who did make a profit. Those who did not lost what they had to those who were productive. They had the wrong idea of stewardship.

The New Testament word which is translated "steward" is *oikonomos*, from which we also get the word, "economy." *Oikos* means "house," and *nemo* means "to arrange." It portrays the concept of administration. What we administer is not ours; it is only entrusted to us.[6]

Beckett also correctly points out that Adam and Eve were set in the garden and then called to steward it. Joseph was brought out of slavery and imprisonment and called to steward Egypt's grain supply so there would be enough food to outlast a devastating drought. The people of Israel were called to steward the law of God; when they did so faithfully, they prospered, and when they didn't, they suffered hardship.

Paul also saw himself as a steward: "Let a man regard us in this manner, as servants of Christ and stewards of the mysteries of God. In this case, moreover, it is required of stewards that one be found trustworthy" (1 Cor. 4:1–2).

This stewardship to which we've been called grows out of the fact that God owns all things. As David wrote, "The earth is the LORD's, and all it contains, the world, and those who dwell in it" (Ps. 24:1). Paul echoed this truth in Romans 11:36: "For from Him and through Him and to Him are all things. To Him be the glory forever. Amen."

We're all stewards. We're stewards of the skills we possess, of the education we've received, of the money we possess, of the products we sell, of the equipment we run and the tools we use, of the people we lead and manage, and of the influence we bring. We're stewards of all that has been entrusted to us. And we answer to God Himself as the owner of all things.

When you see God as your boss and see yourself as a steward of what He owns, your role—whatever it is—takes on great significance. This is why I said earlier that God's calling upon your life has virtually nothing to do with what you do, but everything to do with the perspective with which you do it. Who do you see yourself working for? On whose behalf do you do what you do? If your ultimate boss is your employer, and you carry out your work for the benefit of that employer and your own provision, then your significance will be determined accordingly. The importance of your role—as determined by your employer, the title you answer to, and the pay you receive—will dictate your feelings of significance. If your title isn't highly esteemed and the pay minimal, feelings of significance will be hard to come by.

But since God has made you a steward—a manager of that which is His—it's your job to manage all that you are and all that you have to the glory of His name. When this is truly your perspective, you'll never say again, "I'm just a _____" about anything you do.

I was in late junior high when our family took a trip out West. On the way, we made several sightseeing stops, including the Badlands of South Dakota. It was like journeying back to the days of the Old West. I vividly recall attending a mock trial of an outlaw; I remember it clearly, because my dad was picked out of the audience to be a member of the jury.

He was briefly interviewed in front of all of us by one of the lawyers who was a part of the show. He asked Dad what he did for a living.

"I'm an engineer and manipulator of clay products," he answered.

The lawyer seemed impressed. "Hmm, an engineer, that's good!"

I turned to my mother. "What did Dad say?" I was puzzled by his answer because I knew he was a bricklayer.

She only laughed. "Ask him later."

I did, and Dad explained it: "That's what a bricklayer is—an engineer and manipulator of clay products. It's just a matter of perspective."

A bricklayer isn't a highly esteemed job within our society. As far as significance is concerned, it's pretty low on the scale. And the pay reflects that reality. But my dad didn't see it that way. He saw himself as a craftsman. He took great pleasure in doing a job right, no matter how big or small it was. I cannot tell you how many times I heard during my growing-up years, "If it's worth doing, it's worth doing right." I never heard my dad say, "I'm *just* a bricklayer" or "*just* a blue-collar worker"; he didn't have that perspective or mentality. He saw himself as a steward of what God had entrusted to him.

How You Work

This perspective toward God and toward oneself as a worker makes a difference in one's feelings of significance. It also makes a difference in the way one works.

Paul tells us, "Whatever you do, *do your work heartily,* as for the Lord rather than for men, knowing that from the Lord you will receive the reward of the inheritance. It is the Lord Christ whom you serve" (Col. 3:23–24). It doesn't matter what you do, he says; you need to do it with all your heart. Whether you're the CEO or the receptionist, the professor or the student, the owner of the hotel or someone who cleans the rooms, the one who gets paid millions or nothing at all, the one who takes orders or the one who gives them. Whether you have a corner office, a cubicle, or neither, "whatever you do, do your work heartily."

What do you do with the majority of your day? What's your current primary task? Do you run a business, manage a home, go to school, repair cars, take care of patients, sell a product? *Whatever* it is, do it with all your heart.

Not long ago, I read an outstanding little book titled *The Fred Factor*. Author Mark Sanborn writes of his experiences and the lessons he learned from his mailman, a guy named Fred. The book begins by describing Sanborn's first meeting with the mailman at his new home in Denver:

> "Good morning, Mr. Sanborn!" he said cheerfully, "My name is Fred, and I'm your postal carrier. I just stopped by to introduce myself—to welcome you to the neighborhood and find out a little bit about you and what you do for a living."

> Fred was an ordinary-looking fellow of average height and build with a small mustache. While his physical appearance didn't convey anything out of the ordinary, his sincerity and warmth were noticeable immediately.

> I was a bit startled. Like most of us, I had been receiving mail for years, but I had never had this kind of personal encounter with my postal carrier. I was impressed—nice touch.

> "I'm a professional speaker. I don't have a real job," I replied jokingly.

> "If you're a professional speaker, you must travel a lot," said Fred.

> "Yes, I do. I travel anywhere from 160 to 200 days a year."

Nodding, Fred went on. "Well, if you'll just give me a copy of your schedule, I'll hold your mail and bundle it. I'll only deliver it on the days that you are at home to receive it."

I was amazed by Fred's conscientious offer, but I told him that such extra effort probably wasn't necessary. "Why don't you just leave the mail in the box on the side of the house?" I suggested. "I'll pick it up when I come back into town."

Fred frowned and shook his head. "Mr. Sanborn, burglars often watch for mail building up in a box. That tells them you're out of town. You might become the victim of a break-in." Fred was more worried about my mail than I was! But it made sense; he was the postal professional.

"Here's what I suggest, Mr. Sanborn," Fred continued. "I'll put mail in your box as long as I can get it to close. That way nobody will know you're gone. Whatever doesn't fit in the box, I'll put between the screen door and the front door. Nobody will see it there. And if that area becomes too full of mail, I'll just hold the rest of it for you until you come back into town...."

Two weeks later I returned home from a trip. As I put the key in my front-door lock, I noticed my doormat was missing. Were thieves actually stealing doormats in Denver? Then I saw the mat in a corner of the porch, concealing something. I lifted the mat and found a note from—who else?—Fred! Reading his message, I learned what had happened. While I was gone, a different delivery service had misdelivered a package sent to me. The box had been left on somebody else's porch, five doors down the street. Noticing my box on the wrong porch, Fred had picked it up, carried it to my house, attached his note, and then tried to make the package less noticeable by placing it under the doormat.

Not only was Fred delivering the mail, he was now picking up the slack for UPS![7]

Fred is an example of someone who does work heartily. He embodies three words that I believe capture effort from the heart.

The first word is *passion*. It's the opposite of just going through the motions, putting in your time, getting by, doing the minimum. It's a joy to deal with people who truly have passion for what they do, whatever it may be.

The second word is *excellence*. Paul wrote, "Whether, then, you eat or drink or whatever you do, do all to the glory of God" (1 Cor. 10:31). God is excellent, and that which reflects Him should be excellent as well. This is the opposite of "it's good enough; it'll do."

How many times in your life have you been on the receiving end of "overpromised, underdelivered"? But the one who works with excellence underpromises and overdelivers. And what a joy it is to be on the receiving end of such an effort.

The third word is *integrity*. John Beckett writes,

By definition, *integrity* means adherence to a standard of values. That which is sound, whole, complete has integrity. It can be a bridge structure, a philosophy or a person. The opposite is that which is compromised, fractured, unsound. In the biblical use, the term embraces truthfulness, honesty, uprightness, blamelessness, wholeness.[8]

David writes of integrity in Psalm 15:

O LORD, who may abide in Your tent? Who may dwell on Your holy hill? *He who walks with integrity,* and works righteousness, and speaks truth in his heart. He does not slander with his tongue, nor does evil to his neighbor, nor takes up a reproach against his friend; in whose eyes a reprobate is despised, but who honors those who fear the LORD; he swears to his own hurt and does not change; he does not put out his money at interest; nor does he take a bribe against the innocent. He who does these things will never be shaken.

Beckett continues:

I picture someone who agrees on a handshake to sell a piece of property for a certain sum. The next day another person offers more money. The person of integrity honors the prior commitment, even though backing out would bring greater profit.

This is the student who refuses to cheat in order to obtain a better grade. This is the athlete who walks away from performance-enhancing drugs. This is the taxpaying citizen who reports all cash payments as a part of their income. This is integrity. We're all challenged on some level in some arena to operate with integrity when it appears to be to our advantage to operate otherwise.

The Motivation

Where does the motivation come from to work, in whatever you do, with all your heart?

Paul answers this question by saying we're to work "as for the Lord rather than for men, knowing that from the Lord you will receive the reward of the inheritance. It is the Lord Christ whom you serve" (Col. 3:23–24).

This is such a radical message within our culture today. Our culture tells us that life in all its fullness is found by attaining the American dream: Get a good education ... so you can get a good job ... so you can make a good living ... so you can buy the things you want and feel financially secure. The ultimate goal is to retire as early as possible so you can really do what you want to do, when you want to do it, with whomever you choose. While there's nothing inherently evil in those pursuits, they're misdirected in that they're all aimed at serving "me." Our culture's bible reads, "Whatever you do, do it for yourself." And living like that is completely explainable; that's what most everyone does.

On the other hand, those who do whatever they do as though they answer to God Himself—those who see themselves as a steward and who do their work with all their heart—will set themselves apart from the crowd. Their significance is drawn not from their title, position, or paycheck, but from their calling given by God Himself.

It's rare for all three of these characteristics—passion, excellence, and integrity—to show up in any one person. The humility that comes from seeing yourself as a steward, the dignity that comes from seeing yourself as an ambassador of God, and the quality that results from God-honoring effort—all contribute to an attitude and performance that become unexplainable apart from God.

In return, God grants a sense of significance that the world can't give or take away.

Discussion Questions

1. Were you raised to believe that titles and labels were significant in measuring a person's value?

2. In what ways are you a steward? Explain.

3. What two or three specific examples from recent days can you give to illustrate what it means to "do your work heartily"?

4. Who comes to mind when you think of someone carrying out his or her work with passion, excellence, and integrity?

5. What, if anything, could you do differently so that others would identify *you* as someone who works with passion, excellence, and integrity?

17

YOU ARE GIFTED!

Now concerning spiritual gifts, brethren,
I do not want you to be unaware.

1 CORINTHIANS 12:1

Our family had just emerged from the theater after seeing a Broadway-quality musical when one of my kids exclaimed, "Those are some gifted people." We all agreed.

Gifted is a word we often use to describe those who possess a unique level of ability to do something that the rest of us only dream of being able to do. We speak of gifted musicians—singers, composers, and instrumentalists who leave their audiences shaking their heads in amazement. We speak of gifted athletes—those who possess physical abilities that the rest of us try to emulate but simply can't, no matter how hard we try, train, or practice. We speak of gifted artists as we stand before a painting and simply utter, "Wow!" Magazines display the snapshots of gifted photographers. Large crowds gather to hear gifted communicators. There are also gifted writers, gifted actors, and gifted students.

I remember when our kids were young and we sat together as a family over several evenings reading a book titled *Gifted Hands: The Ben Carson Story.* As one of the world's most renowned pediatric neurosurgeons, Dr. Carson does indeed possess gifted hands.

There are gifted people in virtually every arena of life and field of work—although there's probably a good chance that *you don't count yourself among them.*

Well, if you're a Christian and you think that—you're wrong. You *are* gifted. Just listen to what Paul says about it:

> Now there are varieties of gifts, but the same Spirit. And there are varieties of ministers, and the same Lord. There are varieties of effects, but the same God who works all things in all persons. *But to each one is given the manifestation of the Spirit for the common good.* (1 Cor. 12:4–7)

Were you careful to note that last sentence? The manifestation of the Spirit is given "to each one." If you have a relationship with Jesus, then "each one" includes you.

Paul goes on to list some of these giftings:

> For to one is given the word of wisdom through the Spirit, and to another the word of knowledge according to the same Spirit; to another faith by the same Spirit, and to another gifts of healing by the one Spirit, and to another the effecting of miracles, and to another prophecy, and to another the distinguishing of spirits, to another various kinds of tongues, and to another the interpretation of tongues. (12:8–10)

He then restates the truth we can't afford to miss:

> But one and the same Spirit works all these things, distributing to each one individually just as He wills. (12:11)

The Holy Spirit distributes, as He desires, spiritual gifts *to each and every one* of God's people.

Previously Paul stresses how important it is that we understand this subject: "Now concerning spiritual gifts, brethren, *I do not want you to be unaware*" (12:1). While there are many matters in life that you and I can plead ignorance about, spiritual gifts shouldn't be one of them.

So let's explore the fundamentals of this crucial topic.

What is a spiritual gift?

Spiritual gifts are special abilities given by the Holy Spirit to each and every member of the body of Christ for the benefit of the body. In the simplest of terms, spiritual gifts are supernatural abilities.

Why does God give spiritual gifts to His people?

Looking again at 1 Corinthians 12:7, we read, "But to each one is given the manifestation of the Spirit *for the common good*." God has gifted you so you can make a valued contribution to the body of Christ. By exercising your particular gift or gifts, you make a difference.

God has gifted you so you can be a significant contributor. Can you imagine what your church would be like if every member were actively exercising his or her gifts for the benefit of others in the church?

Unfortunately, the church more often resembles a major sporting event where the vast majority sit in the stands watching and reacting to the minority who are actively participating. This isn't how God intended the church to operate. "Each one" of us should be on the field of play, exercising our gifts for the benefit of the body as a whole. If this were to happen, not only would many needs be met, but the power of God would be on display.

Remember, these gifts are supernatural abilities. Think of it this way: When God gave His Holy Spirit to you, it was as if He placed a powerful twelve-volt battery within. The presence of the Holy Spirit provides you with a power source you can't get any other way. You have the power to say no to temptation, the power to do what's right when it's easier to do what's wrong, and the power to love those who are hard to love and to be patient and kind toward those who need both. Because of the presence of the Holy Spirit, you have the power to love your enemies and to pray for those who persecute you. Because of the Spirit, you have the ability to understand and apply God's truth to your life.

Now let me go one step further. When the Holy Spirit entered your life, He brought along with Him one or more six-volt batteries, intended to help you make a powerful contribution to the body of Christ. These are your spiritual gifts. They represent the manifestation of God's power in your service of others. Spiritual gifts enable you to contribute not merely in your strength, but in God's.

Have you ever wondered why some folks are so effective in making their contribution—perhaps in offering hospitality, or in expressing compassion and mercy, or in sharing the message of Jesus with those outside the family of God, or in teaching the Bible, or in praying over those who are hurting? Perhaps you've wondered why some seem so motivated to help out whenever and wherever a need arises, and others are so quick and motivated to give generously of their resources to meet a need. Well, wonder no more. The reason is this: Spiritual gifts are being exercised.

Do spiritual gifts differ from natural talents?

In a word, yes. The ability to sing, play an instrument, cook, sew, paint, or play a sport with great skill is a talent, not a gift. These talents are similar to gifts in that they're given by God and can be used to bless others. Like gifts, they can be developed and enhanced through practice, and can be used in a way that brings God glory. But they're different from gifts in that all human beings have talent, while only members of the body of Christ possess spiritual gifts.

Spiritual gifts can be expressed through a talent—such as when a talented public speaker is given the gift of teaching, or when a talented musician is given the gift of mercy, or when a talented cook is given the gift of hospitality.

How do I discover my spiritual gifts?

Let me suggest a simple three-step approach for discovering your spiritual gift or gifts (you have at least one, but probably more).

Step 1: Take a spiritual gift assessment. Numerous spiritual gift assessments have been put together to help you get started. There's one in the resource I developed with Bruce Bugbee called *Experiencing LeaderShift Together.* You can also find one in the resource called *Network,* which is devoted to helping believers discover and exercise their spiritual gifts. A man named Peter Wagner has written several books on spiritual gifts and provides this sort of assessment within them.

These assessments are intended only to point you in a direction, and not intended to be the definitive word on your gifting. After taking one of these assessments, you'll probably find that each of the listed gifts falls into one of three categories as it relates to you: (1) those you clearly appear to possess, (2) those you clearly don't appear to possess, and (3) those that fall somewhere in between. I suggest you identify those gifts that are strongly indicated for you, then move to Step 2.

Step 2: Experiment. Try it out. See if it fits. Identify a place of experimentation (more on this in the next chapter). As with natural talents, you discover what you're able to do best by trying it. Most of us discovered natural talents first as children. We took music lessons or signed up to play a sport. In a matter of time, we began to see where our talents lie. Spiritual gifts are no different. Sign up, venture out, give them a try, and see what happens. As you do, move on to Step 3.

Step 3: Seek affirmation. The final "seal of approval" on the gifts you possess is received by the affirmation that comes primarily through three sources.

The first is personal affirmation. There's a blessing that comes to the one who contributes. Do you feel blessed as you serve in this way? Are you experiencing the joy of God—a deeply satisfying sense of fulfillment, an affirming sense of personal worth, a passionate sense of calling? Is this your experience when you exercise these gifts? It should be. You should have a sense that God shows up and expresses Himself through you, for the benefit of someone else or the body as a whole.

Second is the affirmation of others. Hopefully you're serving and exercising your gift or gifts within the context of a team. Rugged individualism may be characteristic of the Old West, but it's not characteristic of the body of Christ. What feedback are you receiving from those who are serving with you? These people may even have the same gifting as you have. Is there strong affirmation from others after your participation, or only a curious silence?

Third is the affirmation of fruit. What results from using your gift? If you have the gift of teaching, you should see people discovering the power of God's truth as you teach. If you have the gift of encouragement, you should find yourself wanting to express encouragement—and finding it natural to do so—and then seeing recipients encouraged as a result. If you have the gift of mercy, then the compassion of God should be flowing through you in a way that lifts others. If God is "in it," there will be fruit— count on it.

This is the definitive form of affirmation. You may initially struggle a bit to define your own experience of God's joy, and those serving with you may be more kind than honest. But fruit doesn't lie. If you have a certain spiritual gift, that fact will be affirmed in the results achieved when you exercise it.

Empowered Contributors

In a world filled with consumers, God has equipped each of His people to be significant contributors—and not just contributors, but supernaturally empowered contributors. You may never be a gifted musician or gifted athlete or gifted artist as the world defines and describes giftedness, but in the kingdom of God, you are gifted. Your gifting isn't intended to leave people amazed at you, but rather amazed at God.

Listen to what Peter writes about this topic of spiritual gifts:

> As each one has received a special gift, employ it in serving one another as good stewards of the manifold grace of God. Whoever speaks, is to do so as one who is speaking the utterances of God; whoever serves is to do so as one who is serving by the strength which God supplies; *so that in all things God may be glorified through Jesus Christ, to whom belongs the glory and dominion forever and ever.* Amen. (1 Peter 4:10–11)

The expression of our spiritual gifts should point others to God. What you contribute and the way you make this contribution should be unexplainable apart from God.

A Personal Story

Before I close this chapter, let me share a personal illustration, for spiritual gifts have played a profound role in my life.

In my junior high years, I had a couple of friends who encouraged me to run for a leadership position on the school student council. While I initially resisted their prodding, eventually I caved in and agreed to run. (I still wonder about their motives; I think they saw me as their meal ticket to get what they wanted.) I filled out the necessary candidate form and turned it in to my teacher.

The next day, I received word that I wouldn't be allowed to run. Apparently too many students had applied, and for reasons not given to me, I wasn't selected as one of the applicants who would be allowed to run.

I informed my parents of the teacher's decision when I got home that afternoon, then went out to play ball. I was actually relieved that I wouldn't be able to run. If by chance I won, I'd be required to take on an up-front role that would call for me to lead meetings and speak in front of groups. Speaking in front of people was way, way down on my list of want-to-dos.

A couple of days later, my teacher pulled me aside and said that things had changed; if I still wanted to run, I could. My friends were again encouraging me. So I agreed.

As it turned out, I won the election. It was only years later that I learned the full details of how it was made possible.

The day after I'd told my parents I wasn't chosen to run, my mother called the principal at the school. She simply wanted some further explanation about the situation. She was invited to meet with the principal and my teacher, who then expressed concern about the negative impact this experience could have on me. They questioned how I would respond if I lost the election. They saw me as shy and reserved, and they questioned my ability to assume a leadership role if I won, knowing of my reluctance to be an up-front guy.

My mother told them she appreciated their concern, but felt this should be my decision, and that I should be allowed to experience the consequences of whatever I decided. She also assured them that, if I lost, she and my dad would take responsibility for how I reacted.

The principal and teacher agreed—and that's why the teacher later approached me to tell me about the change.

Now, many years removed, I'm convinced that God Himself is the primary reason I have the ability to stand before people and teach His Word. In my flesh, I'm a back-row kind of guy. If it weren't for God's gifting me, I'd never feel the need or desire to step onstage in front of others. While it's obvious that some people are "natural" up-front communicators, I don't consider myself all that natural at it. And while other people are naturally strong students—which explains why they embrace hours and hours in the library studying—I was never a fixture at the library.

But I do believe God has given me gifts of leadership and teaching. I resonate with what Paul told the Corinthians: "I was with you in weakness and in fear and in much trembling, and my message and my preaching were not in persuasive words of wisdom, but in demonstration of the Spirit and of power, that your faith would not rest on the wisdom of men, but on the power of God" (1 Cor. 2:3–5).

As I said—unexplainable apart from God.

Pointing the Way

So let me ask you:

> *How has God gifted you?*
>
> *What contribution has He called you to make with your gifts?*
>
> *How dependent are you upon the "demonstration of the Spirit and of power"?*
>
> *What do you do that you know is unexplainable apart from God?*

The answer to these questions will help point you to a truly significant contribution.

In turn, when you see God display Himself through you and the blessing that comes to others as a result, there's a resulting fulfillment that you can get no other way.

No title, no position, no paycheck, and no applause from others will ever be able to equal the sense of significance that God grants to those who become vessels of His power. To see God worshipped by those He has used you to serve is a measure of significance that the world cannot bestow.

So, I urge you, discover how God has gifted you. Exercise your gifts and make a truly significant contribution.

Discussion Questions

1. Is there anything you learned about spiritual gifts that you didn't know before reading this chapter?

2. To what degree does the church you attend utilize spiritual gifts in determining how people serve? (Answer *none at all, somewhat,* or *to a great degree.*)

3. Do you know what your spiritual gifts are? If so, what are they, and how did you come to know that these are your gifts? If you don't know your spiritual gifts, what steps can you take to discover them?

4. To what degree are you currently using your spiritual gifts in the body of Christ? (Answer *not at all, somewhat,* or *completely.* If somewhat or completely, explain what you do.)

18

GOD-GIVEN PASSION

But now faith, hope, love, abide these three;
but the greatest of these is love.

1 CORINTHIANS 13:13

One of my all-time favorite quotes is from John Wesley: "Catch on fire with enthusiasm, and people will come for miles to watch you burn."

In a day and age when so many people are merely going through the motions of life, those with passion do indeed stand out. And they're the ones who end up making the most significant contribution. As someone once said, "Enthusiasm (passion) can achieve more in one day than what it takes reason to do in centuries."

One of the most famous chapters in the Bible is 1 Corinthians 13, known as the love chapter. Even if you'd never read the Bible personally, chances are you'd be familiar with 1 Corinthians 13 simply as a result of attending weddings or receiving greeting cards. Have you ever stopped to consider why this treatise on love is located where it is in the Bible? I don't think its location is insignificant. I think God placed it where it is for a reason.

The preceding chapter—1 Corinthians 12—is all about spiritual gifts and the role they play in the body of Christ, as we explored earlier. Meanwhile, in 1 Corinthians 14, Paul again addresses the matter of spiritual gifts and their use and misuse in the body of Christ. Sandwiched in between these two chapters on spiritual gifts is this portrait of love in 1 Corinthians 13.

A professional editor would probably rearrange all that. He'd put the content of chapters 12 and 14 side by side, then perhaps follow it with the content on love. But that isn't how God arranged it—for good reason.

I believe God wanted to make it clear that *love is the glue that holds the body of Christ together.* It's when spiritual gifts are expressed *in love* that they truly make their intended contribution.

Listen to Paul's opening words in this love chapter:

> If I speak with the tongues of men and of angels, but do not have love, I have become a noisy gong or a clanging cymbal. If I have the gift of prophecy, and know all mysteries and all knowledge; and if I have all faith, so as to remove mountains, but do not have love, I am nothing. And if I give all my possessions to feed the poor, and if I surrender my body to be burned, but do not have love, it profits me nothing. (13:1–3)

Take love out of the picture, and *there is no picture.* Spiritual gifts expressed without love accomplish nothing. Love must be the motivation behind the expression of every gift. Love is the glue that holds the body of Christ together.

Paul then defines and describes what love is:

> Love is patient, love is kind and is not jealous; love does not brag and is not arrogant, does not act unbecomingly; it

does not seek its own, is not provoked, does not take into account a wrong suffered, does not rejoice in unrighteousness, but rejoices with the truth; bears all things, believes all things, hopes all things, endures all things. Love never fails; but if there are gifts of prophecy, they will be done away; if there are tongues, they will cease; if there is knowledge, it will be done away. (13:4–8)

In the event that his readers still fail to understand the priority of love, Paul concludes the chapter this way:

But now faith, hope, love, abide these three; but the greatest of these is love. (13:13)

Is love greater than faith and more important than hope? Yes, absolutely.

It's impossible to talk about a God-anointed contribution apart from love. The apostle John wrote this about love:

The one who does not love does not know God, for God is love. By this the love of God was manifested in us, that God has sent His only begotten Son into the world so that we might live through Him. In this is love, not that we loved God, but that He loved us and sent His Son to be the propitiation for our sins. Beloved, if God so loved us, we also ought to love one another. No one has seen God at any time; if we love one another, God abides in us, and His love is perfected in us. (1 John 4:8–12)

Love is the mark of distinction. As Jesus said to His disciples on the night before He was crucified,

A new commandment I give to you, that you love one
another, even as I have loved you, that you also love one
another. By this all men will know that you are My disciples, if you have love for one another. (John 13:34–35)

At the Core

Love is at the very foundation of the Christian's life. Do you recall the
lawyer who came to Jesus one day asking Him to identify the greatest commandment in all the law? Jesus answered him this way:

"You shall love the Lord your God with all your heart, and
with all your soul, and with all your mind." This is the
great and foremost commandment. The second is like it,
"You shall love your neighbor as yourself." On these two
commandments depend the whole Law and the Prophets.
(Matt. 22:37–40)

My friend, *this is passion*—loving the Lord with all your heart, soul,
and mind. There's no "going through the motions" here. There's to be nothing halfhearted about our love for God. And this passion of ours flows in
response to God's passion toward us.

Listen again to John's statement: "We love, because He first loved us"
(1 John 4:19). Is it any mystery why the word *passion* is used in reference
to the suffering of Christ between the night of the Last Supper and His
death? And what title would have been more fitting for a movie depicting
this period than *The Passion of the Christ*? Jesus wasn't going through the
motions. There was nothing halfhearted or lukewarm about Him giving
His life.

God-given passion is based on and in God's love.

This is different from the passion of this world. Just yesterday, a friend said to me, "I love college football." I didn't need an interpreter or any further clarification to understand what he was saying; he's *passionate* about college football.

We all understand this sort of passion. Since moving to west Michigan, I've met many men who are passionate about hunting. While I don't share their passion, I can clearly see it.

I have a relative who's a passionate Chicago Bears fan. I'm a Bears fan too, but he's *passionate*—and there's a difference.

These passions and many others like them are based upon personal pleasure. We're passionate about things we enjoy. We're passionate about involvements that "do something" for us. We receive enjoyment, or relaxation, or a thrill from that which we're passionate about. And this is good. As Paul wrote, "God … richly supplies us with all things to enjoy" (1 Tim. 6:17).

But the passion of which I'm writing is a God-given passion. This passion flows from God's love. It's the expression of God's love through us. God-given passion doesn't revolve around personal pleasure. It's rather a reflection of the love of God, and it expresses itself in service to others. This love-motivated service should be passionate in its expression. And when it is, the only explanation is God.

In the dictionary, passion is defined as an "intense, driving, or overmastering feeling or conviction," "ardent affection," "love," and "a strong liking or desire for or devotion to some activity, object, or concept." Based on that, Christians should be the most passionate of people. And the body of Christ, regardless of the specific church or organization, should be bursting at the seams with passion. No people should feel or display greater passion than those who have received and experienced the love of God.

And as God's love touches us and is expressed through us, it's expressed in God-given passion for that which God loves. I've seen this passion in God's people.

Some of them are convinced that children's ministry is the most important endeavor on the face of the earth. They genuinely believe that children are not only the most receptive audience but the most important audience to reach with the good news of Jesus Christ. These people seem to carry the love of God for children in their hearts.

I've been around others who display a similar passion for student ministry. They see adolescence as the critical time of life. "Children are a bit young," they'll say, "and adults are a bit old."

I've met others who see the ages of eighteen to thirty as the most spiritually critical period, since so many life-shaping decisions like career and marriage are typically made in this season of life.

Of course, if you talk with those involved in family ministry, they'll remind you that the foundation of all of society and all of life is the family, and that the family that operates according to God's design will raise healthy children who choose to follow Jesus and make decisions that honor Him. Therefore, they say, no ministry could be more important, or closer to the heart of God, than that which helps strengthen marriages and trains parents to parent effectively.

Others have their own passion area that they claim to be the one closest to the heart of God.

Those who come alongside the hurting point out what Jesus read when He entered the temple and read Scripture for the first time:

> The Spirit of the Lord is upon Me, because He anointed Me to preach the gospel to the poor. He has sent Me to proclaim release to the captives, and recovery of sight to the blind, to see free those who are oppressed, to proclaim the favorable year of the Lord. (Luke 4:18–19)

While they make a strong case, it's equally difficult to argue with those who quote these words of Jesus: "My house shall be called a house of prayer." These prayer-team folks are quick to say, "When we work, we work, but when we pray, God works." It's hard to say that anything's more important within the life of the church than prayer, and I've known many who believe this passionately.

But the worship-team people say the same thing about their ministry. As they see it, prayer is a subset of the overarching purpose of life, which is to glorify God. These folks boldly ask, "What's more important to God than worship?"

At which point the Bible teachers step forward and ask, "And how do you know what's important to God? How do you really know who God is, and how to best relate to Him, apart from His written Word?" These teachers are quick to point out that the only way we know what Jesus taught on prayer, and what He read when He first entered the temple, is through His recorded Word. Therefore, they say, "Nothing's more important than the teaching of the Bible."

About this time the missions people and the evangelists among us step forward and say, "Lost souls—that's what matters most." They point out that Jesus would have already returned by now were it not for God's desire "for all to come to repentance" (2 Peter 3:9); God the Father is patiently waiting for more to come to repentance, and therefore nothing is more important than the proclamation of the good news of Jesus Christ.

A Piece of God's Heart

So what really is most important?

If you're involved in one of the ministries I just mentioned, your answer is probably that one. If I haven't mentioned the ministry you're involved in, you're probably wondering how I could possibly overlook it.

Which one's *really* most important? The correct answer is—all of them! God is passionately—yes, *passionately*—concerned about every ministry I mentioned, and many more I didn't mention.

God also understands that we don't possess the capacity of heart that He does. Nor do we have the time and energy to be passionate about all that He is. So it appears that God gives each of His people a piece of His heart—a God-given passion—for some specific dimension of His work. God's love invades a human heart, and that heart—with its limited capacity and scope—begins to passionately love something that God loves.

I met a man recently who's absolutely passionate about serving Native Americans in the name of Jesus. Recently, I spent an afternoon with a young man who feels called of God to reach inner-city youth. One night on the ten o'clock news, I listened to a man speak passionately about the mission he ran for the purpose of getting homeless people off the streets where they were in danger of starving or freezing to death.

While God's love should clearly be on display within and through the body of Christ, it's certainly not limited to that setting. I have several friends who know they're led of God to the marketplace where they passionately work to express God's love to others. While committed to their respective business involvements, they're even more committed to being agents of God's love in the world in which God has placed them. I know of athletic coaches who are passionate about impacting young people, and athletics is the connection that provides an opportunity for such an impact. It has been my privilege over the past couple of years to work with a team of people at David C. Cook who are passionate about bringing God's life-changing truth to people all over the world; in their case, the Christian publishing industry serves as a platform for their passion.

Finding Your Passion

How about you? How is God's heart being expressed through your heart? What's your God-given passion?

If you know the answer to that, I trust you're pursuing it passionately.

If you *don't* know the answer, let me suggest a couple of action steps you can take in order to find out:

Step 1: Pray. Ask God to give you a passion. Ask Him to put a piece of His heart in your heart. Ask Him to give you His love for something, for some group of people, for some cause, for some endeavor, that will enable Him to express His love through you. This is a prayer He'll surely answer.

Step 2: Take a passion assessment. Perhaps you need a little assistance, some ideas to get you going, some direction to get you started. You can find a passion assessment in two resources I mentioned earlier, *Experiencing LeaderShift Together* and *Network.* Such a passion assessment can help you identify the passion God has already placed in your heart.

Step 3: Get involved. Take a step. Try something on for size, and see if it fits. By getting involved in a specific ministry, you can discover if something stirs in your heart.

Believe me when I say, God has no interest in seeing His people merely going through the motions. While we may occasionally need to be willing to do something we are not passionate about, doing something out of duty or a sense of obligation is *not* what God desires. So step out and get involved in something for which you think you may have a passion. See what happens. See how God expresses His love through you.

You'll know you've landed on your God-given passion when your involvement becomes unexplainable apart from Him.

A Shared Passion

For the past couple of years, I've been associated with a ministry called City on a Hill. A local hospital was relocated to a new facility across town. As a result, the old facility was put up for sale. A small group of God's people had a vision to make that facility a center for ministry. After much prayer and discussion, their vision was cast to the larger Christian community.

That larger Christian community bought the facility, and today it houses about thirty different ministries.

While these ministries come in all different shapes and sizes, they all have one thing in common—a God-given passion to bring the love of God in a tangible way to some specific group of people in need. Visit City on a Hill Ministries and you'll find some people with a God-given passion for children with special needs. You'll find others who are passionate about helping those who are in bondage to some sort of addiction. Others have a God-given passion to supply food and clothing to those in need and still others offer medical services free of charge to those who can't afford them.

Why do they do it? What's the explanation for such passion? Will they become famous? Probably not. Will they become wealthy? Certainly not. There's only one explanation—God. His love has permeated their hearts and is now spilling out in love for others. And the end result is that many are being pointed to God.

So let me ask: What piece of God's heart do you carry? How is His love being expressed through your life? Are you involved in making a significant contribution for which the only explanation is God?

If not, you're missing out. True significance is felt when you see God pouring His life through your life in a way that makes a lasting difference.

Ask God to give you a piece of His heart for this broken world. When He does, you'll begin to display a passion that is unexplainable apart from God.

Discussion Questions

1. What would those closest to you say you are passionate about?
2. Who comes to mind when you think of God-given passion? Explain what you see in them.
3. What "piece of God's heart" do you carry? Explain. If you don't know yet, what steps can you take to find out?
4. In what ways is God's love being expressed through your life?

19

THE ANOINTING OF GOD

"Not by might nor by power, but by My
Spirit," says the LORD of hosts.

ZECHARIAH 4:6

The Bible is a running record of God doing the unexplainable.

Take, for example, the life of David. We're first introduced to David when he becomes the unexplainable choice of God (in 1 Sam. 16) to be the next king of Israel, as we looked at earlier. God used that choice of David to remind the prophet Samuel (and us) that "God sees not as man sees, for man looks at the outward appearance, but the LORD looks at the heart."

This truth about the heart is usually where the emphasis is placed when this well-known story is taught. And while that emphasis is certainly significant, a perhaps even more important truth is seen in what happens when God finds the heart He's looking for:

> Then Samuel took the horn of oil and anointed him
> in the midst of his brothers; and *the Spirit of the LORD*

came mightily upon David from that day forward. (1 Sam.
16:13)

Right after this anointing, the famous event of the very next chapter
occurs: David kills the great Philistine warrior Goliath. When the story of
David and Goliath is taught, emphasis is typically placed on David's great
faith and his deep concern for God's reputation. While both are evident,
neither is the secret behind David's ability to defeat Goliath. The secret is
back in 1 Samuel 16:13: "The Spirit of the LORD came mightily upon David
from that day forward." David—God's unexplainable choice—now did an
unexplainable thing in defeating Goliath. The power of God, through His
Holy Spirit, is the only explanation.

The anointing of God brings the power of God—so that what takes place
can be explained only by God's participation.

The Source of Power

Now let's fast-forward a thousand years to the opening of the New Testament
and the life and ministry of Jesus Himself:

> Now when all the people were baptized, Jesus was also
> baptized, and while He was praying, heaven was opened,
> and the Holy Spirit descended upon Him in bodily form
> like a dove, and a voice came out of heaven, "You are My
> beloved Son, in You I am well-pleased." When He began
> His ministry, Jesus Himself was about thirty years of age.
> (Luke 3:21–23)

Jesus' baptism served as the launching of His public ministry. But
immediately following His baptism, He was led to the wilderness for a time
of testing:

> Jesus, full of the Holy Spirit, returned from the Jordan
> and was led around by the Spirit in the wilderness for
> forty days, being tempted by the devil. (Luke 4:1–2).

There Jesus underwent a severe time of testing, which He passed with flying colors. How was He able to resist such compelling temptations? Let me return to Luke 4:1, but this time making a slight adjustment:

> And Jesus returned from the Jordan and was led around by
> the Spirit in the wilderness for forty days, being tempted
> by the devil.

Did you notice what I changed? I left out only one short phrase. My omission doesn't impact the flow of the verse—but it certainly impacts the outcome of the temptations.

The phrase I removed was "full of the Holy Spirit." *That* is the reason Jesus was able to resist three incredibly compelling temptations. The power of God coming through Him is the explanation for His victory.

Continuing in Luke 4, we read:

> And Jesus returned to Galilee in the power of the Spirit,
> and news about Him spread through all the surrounding
> district. And He began teaching in their synagogues and
> was praised by all. (Luke 4:14–15)

Why was the news about Jesus spreading? Why was His teaching being praised by all who heard Him?

When Luke wrote those two verses above, he could have simply written, "And Jesus returned to Galilee; and news about Him spread through all the surrounding district. And He began teaching in their synagogues and was praised by all." If we read or heard it that way, most of us wouldn't think twice about its accuracy. But it wouldn't be accurate because of the importance of the missing phrase: "in the power of the Spirit." It was the Spirit who made what Jesus said and did so remarkable.

Jesus next entered the synagogue, where the book of the prophet Isaiah was handed to Him. Luke writes,

> And He opened the book and found the place where it was written, "The Spirit of the Lord is upon Me, because He anointed Me." (Luke 4:17–18)

Of all the passages Jesus could have read when He first entered the synagogue, this was the one scheduled for reading. The first words out of His mouth speak of the "anointing of God." Jesus knew the source of His power: the anointing of the Spirit of the Lord.

This anointing was clearly evident throughout His ministry, as Peter later recalled:

> You know of Jesus of Nazareth, how *God anointed Him with the Holy Spirit and with power,* and how He went about doing good and healing all who were oppressed by the devil, for God was with Him. (Acts 10:38)

Now fast-forward once again, about three and a half years. The passage is Acts 1, and we see Jesus standing with a small group of followers, just forty days removed from His resurrection. They didn't know it at the time, but He was going to give them final instructions and then ascend into heaven.

> Gathering them together, He commanded them not to leave Jerusalem, but to wait for what the Father had

promised, "Which," He said, "you heard of from Me."
(Acts 1:4)

As it turned out, He didn't give them multiple instructions, but
an instruction—just one. They were "to wait for what the Father had
promised."

Jesus went on to add this promise: "You will be baptized with the Holy
Spirit" (1:5). And this one: "You will receive power when the Holy Spirit
has come upon you" (1:8). And when He'd finished speaking of the Holy
Spirit, He ascended into heaven.

Given the circumstances of that day—the fact that He was leaving for
good—plus His command that they be His witnesses "even to the remotest
part of the earth" (1:8), giving them only *one* instruction seems to fall woefully short of what His followers needed.

To put it in perspective, let me draw a comparison. When our three
children were very young and we would leave them in the hands of a
babysitter for an evening, MaryAnn would give the sitter more than
one instruction, even though we were coming back in only a couple
of hours. On the rare occasion when we were going to be gone overnight, MaryAnn would leave a page or two full of instructions (usually
for Grandma and Grandpa). Yet in Acts 1, Jesus is leaving *for good*—
and all He says is, "Wait for the Holy Spirit." It wasn't even an action
instruction.

His followers chose to obey this single instruction, and ten days later,
the Holy Spirit came. With the Spirit came the power of God "to be witnesses for Jesus in Jerusalem, in all Judea, and Samaria, and even to the
remotest parts of the earth."

The disciples' experience proved that all they needed was that one
instruction. Without the Holy Spirit, there was no action to take; with the
Holy Spirit, subsequent actions would unfold by the power of God.

Paul's Anointing

Now, let's fast-forward again to the life and ministry of the apostle Paul, who himself was unexplainable apart from God. The role that the anointing of God played in life is repeatedly made clear:

> I was with you in weakness and in fear and in much trembling, and my message and my preaching were not in persuasive words of wisdom, but *in demonstration of the Spirit and of power*, so that your faith would not rest on the wisdom of men, *but on the power of God.* (1 Cor. 2:3–5)

> But we have this treasure in earthen vessels, so that the surpassing greatness of the power will be of God and not from ourselves. (2 Cor. 4:7)

> We proclaim Him, admonishing every man and teaching every man with all wisdom, so that we may present every man complete in Christ. For this purpose also I labor, *striving according to His power, which mightily works within me.* (Col. 1:28–29)

> For our gospel did not come to you in word only, *but also in power and in the Holy Spirit* and with full conviction; just as you know what kind of men we proved to be among you for your sake. (1 Thess. 1:5)

Paul was under no illusions as to who supplied the power for his life and ministry.

Experiencing the Anointing

Once more time, let's fast-forward—about two thousand years this time, to your own life. Are you experiencing the anointing of God? Is the power of God flowing through you in such a way that the only explanation for your contribution is God?

This is God's desire for you. He wants to anoint your efforts for several reasons.

- *He wants to put Himself on display through you.*

He wants others to look at you and see Him. As Peter wrote,

> Whoever speaks is to do so as one who is speaking the utterances of God; whoever serves is to do so as one who is serving by the strength which God supplies; *so that in all things God may be glorified through Jesus Christ,* to whom belongs the glory and dominion forever and ever. Amen. (1 Peter 4:11)

If you can make your contribution apart from the need for God's power, then your contribution is explainable. If, however, your contribution is made in the demonstration of God's power, then your contribution is unexplainable apart from God.

- *He wants to bring His influence into the world through you.*

God loves the world and wants the world to know it. He wants you to possess a power far beyond your own in order to bring His influence to the world in which you live. He wants to make a difference through you. His power in and through you brings His significant influence.

- *He wants to bless you.*

He wants to bless you by filling your heart with His presence, and filling your life with the manifestation of His power.

God isn't looking to "use" you for someone else's benefit. You aren't merely a means to an end. He gives you spiritual gifts so you'll have His power to make a valued contribution. He gives you a piece of His heart—a God-given passion—so that what you do is a want-to, not merely a have-to. He gives you a unique personality, as well as strengths and talents. He brings into your path opportunities for good works that enable you to feel your inestimable worth.

He gives you all these things as blessings—and perhaps greatest of all, He gives you His indwelling presence. As Jesus said,

> If you then, being evil, know how to give good gifts to your children, how much more will your heavenly Father give the Holy Spirit to those who ask Him? (Luke 11:13)

Your heavenly Father wants to give you the gift of His Holy Spirit. He wants you to live with the power of the Spirit. And with that power, He wants you to make a significant contribution that's a blessing not only to others, but to yourself.

So let me ask: Where does the power of God seem to flow through your life? In what you do, when does it seem that God "shows up"? What is it that causes you to say in reflection, "God made me to do that!"

I think of Eric Liddell, the great runner whose story is told in the movie *Chariots of Fire*. When his sister did her best to get Eric to quit running so he could devote more time to what really mattered—their family's mission work—Eric defended his athletic involvement. "God made me fast," he told her. "And when I run, I feel His pleasure."

Eric Liddell's God-given athletic ability provided him with a platform from which to proclaim the name of Jesus. As a result, he didn't see running as a frivolous pursuit, but rather as a means of making a contribution to the work of the kingdom.

In much the same way, God has given you the ability to make an anointed contribution. And like Eric Liddell, you should be able to say, "This is who God made me to be, and what God gave me the ability to do—and when I do it, *I feel His pleasure.*"

Do you know what that is for you? Discovering your spiritual gifts will help point you in the right direction. When your gifts are exercised in an arena of God-given passion, the presence and power of God will be released in a way and to a degree that makes your contribution one of true significance.

God may enable you to utilize one of your natural talents as He did with Eric Liddell. God may put your formal education to use as well as a skill you've developed. God wants to give you the joy of taking everything He's called you to be and applying it all to the contribution He has called you to make.

I encourage you to set aside some time to quiet yourself before the Lord and to ask Him to help you write down how you would complete these statements:

God made me ...

And I feel His pleasure when I ...

I have a friend who would answer this way: "God made me a business-man, and I feel His pleasure when I generate a profit and use it to bring God glory." This friend has come to understand that God didn't give him the ability to make money in order to increase his standard of living, but rather to increase his standard of giving. This understanding has come to him as he has embraced his true calling, which is to do life in response to his relationship with Jesus.

I've watched this friend grow spiritually from his days as a young follower of Jesus. I've seen his passion to know and follow Jesus increase over time. He believes that God prepared him, even before he became a Christian, for the business he engages in today. As a result, he sees his work as a calling. God is his boss, and he's a steward of all that God has entrusted to him. He does what he does with all his heart, and it's expressed through passion, excellence, and integrity.

He has also taken steps to discover his spiritual gifts. He's now using these gifts for the good of the body of Christ. He has identified specific ministries for which he feels passionate. I call this an anointed life.

Such a life is what God has created you and me to experience as well. It's what we all want—a life of true significance.

The world cannot give you an anointed life. Nor can it give you the sense of significance that comes from being a recipient of God's anointing. An anointed life is unattainable, and unexplainable, apart from God.

Discussion Questions

1. Can you recall a time when the Holy Spirit very clearly expressed His power through you (the anointing of the Holy Spirit)? Explain.

2. Fill in the blanks: God made me _____, and I feel His pleasure when I _____.

3. To what degree does your life as a whole reflect the use of your spiritual gifts in an area of God-given passion? (Answer *not at all, somewhat,* or *completely.*) Explain.

4. What could you change or do differently to increase the anointing of the Holy Spirit in your life overall?

PART FOUR

FROM EXPLAINABLE
TO UNEXPLAINABLE

How to Get There

20

LET GO AND LET GOD

*Therefore I urge you, brethren, by the mercies of God, to
present your bodies a living and holy sacrifice, acceptable
to God, which is your spiritual service of worship.*

ROMANS 12:1

The benefits that come from living an unexplainable-apart-from-God life reflect the fulfillment of Jesus' words found in John 10:10: "I came that they may have life, and have it abundantly."

The abundance of which Jesus spoke is not the health and wealth that some claim it is. It is instead the satisfaction of the deepest longings found within the human heart.

Which of us doesn't long to be content—truly content? What would you give to be forever freed from feelings of dissatisfaction, anxiety, and agitation? What would you pay for inner peace that transcends "outside" conditions and circumstances? This is the abundance to which Jesus refers.

In the same way, which of us doesn't long to be a success in a way that counts forever? Is there not something in your heart that causes you to want to say, as Paul did, "I have fought the good fight, I have finished the course, I have kept the faith; in the future there is laid up for me the crown of righteousness, which the Lord, the righteous Judge, will award to me on that day; and not only to me, but also to all who have loved His appearing" (2 Tim. 4:7–8)? Such sentiments at the end of one's life scream "Abundance!"

And which of us doesn't crave significance, to know that we matter, that we count, that we are valued for who we are and not just for what we do? These longings, found in every human heart, were placed there by God Himself. He placed them there with the hope that we would search for Him, the only source of their satisfaction and fulfillment. I think of the words God spoke through the prophet Jeremiah:

> "For I know the plans that I have for you," declares the
> LORD, "plans for welfare and not for calamity to give you
> a future and a hope. Then you will call upon Me and come
> and pray to Me, and I will listen to you. You will seek Me
> and find Me when you search for Me with all your heart."
> (Jer. 29:11–13)

Only God, our Designer and Creator, can meet the deepest longings of our heart. Only He can provide the peace "which surpasses all comprehension." Only He can lead us to the kind of success that lasts forever. And only in Him can we realize and experience our true worth as those made in His image.

The apostle Paul understood this fact of "only God," as evidenced in these words: "For to me, to live is Christ and to die is gain" (Phil. 1:21). The apostle Peter understood this fact of "only God," as evidenced by his response one day to Jesus: "Lord, to whom shall we go? You have words of eternal life" (John 6:68). Oh that you and I would understand too that "only God" can give us what we crave most.

So why don't we search for God with all our heart? Why don't we look to Him as though He were the only source of true abundance?

Believing a Lie

In the simplest of terms, there are two explanations for why we pursue abundant life apart from God.

The first explanation is our fallen nature. Sin impacts us. It has marred our judgment. Our ability to receive and understand truth is warped by our sinful condition. Imperfect people think imperfect thoughts and therefore make imperfect judgments that result in wrong pursuits.

As Solomon wrote, "There is a way which seems right to a man, but its end is the way of death" (Prov. 16:25). Apart from God, we don't know the way to go. We do what seems right to us and are so often wrong.

Sin has also altered our desires. We crave the gifts instead of the Giver. We look to the things of the world to satisfy "the lust of the flesh and the lust of the eyes and the boastful pride of life" (1 John 2:16). Our sinful nature leads us astray.

The second explanation is that we have believed the Enemy's lies that we can find satisfaction for our heart's longings through the things of this world. The Enemy tells us that we can find contentment by getting all the outside conditions and circumstances of life to be as we want them to be. He says that by pursuing the satisfaction of everything on your "if-only" list, you can be free of dissatisfaction, anxiety, and agitation. Even though God, through His Word, tells us in no uncertain terms that the Enemy is lying and that such a pursuit will never produce contentment, we choose to believe the Enemy.

What results is the roller coaster of emotions that we experience as the conditions and circumstances of life change. Dissatisfaction, anxiety, and agitation become the common experience for almost everyone.

In a different way, the Enemy uses the world to seduce us into believing that abundant life comes through achieving worldly success. Have what you want, do what you want, experience what you desire, achieve control over today as well as tomorrow—this is abundant life, he says. Money, of course, is the primary means to achieve such control and to enjoy such comfort.

Again, God tells us that our Enemy is lying. Success as the world defines it is temporary and superficial. It will satisfy the longings of your flesh but not the longings of your heart. In the end, you'll only hear God say, "You fool! This very night your soul is required of you, and now who will own what you have prepared?" All of your eternity will be impacted as a result. The Enemy is content to give you success in this world, for he knows it doesn't satisfy, it won't last, and most importantly, it brings God no glory.

Finally, the Enemy plays on our longing for significance and tells us that we'll find it through the admiration-filled eyes of others. We look around and see those who appear to be significant because of what they've achieved, accomplished, attained, or accumulated, and we conclude that we should achieve, accomplish, attain, or accumulate the same. This sort of worldly significance is built on what we *do,* not on who we *are.* It therefore falls woefully short of satisfying the longing of our heart for true significance.

Our sinful nature makes us susceptible to the lies of the Enemy.

What Are We to Do?

In this book's first chapter, I told you I was going to encourage and challenge you to make three major adjustments in the way you see and approach life—three lifeshifts. I believe this is exactly what the apostle Paul is instructing us to do in Romans 12:2. Listen again to his words:

> Do not be conformed to this world, but be transformed
> by the renewing of your mind, so that you may prove
> what the will of God is, that which is good and acceptable
> and perfect.

Paul couldn't have stated the truth any more simply or plainly than he does here. *Do not be conformed to this world*—don't buy the lies of the Enemy; the ways of the world will never satisfy the longings of your heart for contentment, success, or significance, nor will they ever give you abundant life, no matter how much you gain. *Be transformed by the renewing of your mind*—your imperfect thoughts and imperfect judgment and fleshly desires must be and can be renewed and transformed. How? By *the will of God, that which is good and acceptable and perfect.*

I've sought to fill this book with the Word of God. It is the Word of God that captures and communicates the will of God. The renewal of your mind will occur as the Word of God washes over it and dwells within it. As Jesus said so simply, "You will know the truth, and the truth will make you free" (John 8:32).

You and I must know God's truth. It is His truth that renews and transforms our sin-impacted minds. It is His truth that enables us to expose and overcome the lies of the Enemy. We need to follow the example of Jesus who responded to the deceit-filled temptations of the Enemy with the words "It is written." If we're going to experience the kind of contentment and success and significance for which our hearts long, we'll need to embrace God's truth and obey God's will.

Is Truth Enough?

Having stated the all-important role of God's truth in our lives, I now need to state clearly that truth alone is not enough. God has not called us to truth; He has called us to Himself! The ultimate goal is not to know truth, but to know Him. The Christian life doesn't flow from information; it flows from relationship. To know God's truth about contentment, success, and significance is critically important, but knowing the truth about those pursuits will not take us to the place of experiencing them. Only God, in relationship with us, can turn that truth into experience.

Those words of command in Romans 12:2 about our being transformed and renewed follow immediately after this appeal from Paul:

> Therefore I urge you, brethren, by the mercies of God, to
> present your bodies a living and holy sacrifice, acceptable
> to God, which is your spiritual service of worship. (12:1)

It's only right and fitting that Paul starts with this foundational truth: You and the unfolding of your life are to be an expression of *worship* to God. You were created to point to Him.

In the final section of this book, I want to respond directly to this question: How do I journey toward a life that is unexplainable apart from God? How do I become someone for whom there's only one explanation: "God did it."

I've answered this question in part as I've presented God's truth. With the foundation of His truth in clear view, it's now necessary to see how that truth can become our personal experience as a result of our relationship with God, since He sent His Son to the earth not so that we could know truth, but so that we could know Him. As you grab hold of God's hand and follow Him, He will lead you in ways that are beyond you. He will take you to places you can't get to without Him. He'll do things in you and through you that are explainable only by the words, "God did it."

This relationship begins with submission before God. As Paul said, "Present your bodies a living and holy sacrifice." Have you surrendered your life to Him? Have you submitted your will to His will? Have you invited God to lead you in the way you should go? Have you said to Him, "I want it *your* way"? God won't force you to live for Him. He has given you the freedom to choose whether you want your life to point to yourself or to Him; whether you want to live within the restricted boundaries of the explainable or the limitless expanses of the unexplainable.

For your sake, I encourage you to submit yourself before Him; to let go of the reins of your life and let God take over. He designed and created you to point to Him, and when you do, the deepest longings of your heart will be satisfied.

Paul spoke in 1 Corinthians 2:9 about "things which eye has not seen and ear has not heard, and which have not entered the heart of man, all that God has prepared for those who love Him." He will lead you into "all that He has prepared for you" as you *relate* to Him. You'll need to learn to (1) hear His voice, (2) walk by faith, and (3) depend upon His grace. It's with these three topics that I'll conclude this book.

Discussion Questions

1. What parts of your sinful nature make you most vulnerable to the lies of the Enemy?

2. What lies about contentment, success, and significance are you most likely to accept as true? Explain.

3. What truths do you most need to know, embrace, and obey in order to dispel the effects of the Enemy's lies? Try to identify a specific verse or passage that states this truth.

4. Is it difficult for you to submit yourself before God? If so, why?

21

ARE YOU LISTENING?

My sheep hear My voice, and I know
them, and they follow Me.

JOHN 10:27

The basis of any valued and meaningful relationship is two-way communication. Both talking and listening are required. Where one party does all the talking and the other all the listening, the relationship is severely lacking.

This is true in any relationship, including yours with God.

Most of us understand talking to God; we refer to it as prayer. What we don't understand nearly as well is listening to Him. Somehow we've come to believe that we can have a meaningful relationship with God even if we do the talking and He the listening.

Nothing could be further from the truth. God wants a relationship with you—two-way communication, talking *and* listening. In fact, prayer is every bit as much listening as it is talking. As we listen to God, He leads us in the way we're to go. Therefore, we must learn how to listen, and how to recognize the voice of the Lord.

Get Yourself in Position to Hear

The story of the boy Samuel serves as a good example of why some of us are unable to hear.

> Now the boy Samuel was ministering to the LORD before Eli. And word from the LORD was rare in those days, visions were infrequent.
>
> It happened at that time as Eli was lying down in his place (now his eyesight had begun to grow dim and he could not see well), and the lamp of God had not yet gone out, and Samuel was lying down in the temple of the LORD where the ark of God was, that the LORD called Samuel; and he said, "Here I am." Then he ran to Eli and said, "Here I am, for you called me."
>
> But he said, "I did not call, lie down again."
>
> So he went and lay down. The LORD called yet again, "Samuel!" So Samuel arose and went to Eli and said, "Here I am, for you called me."
>
> But he answered, "I did not call, my son, lie down again." Now Samuel did not yet know the LORD, nor had the word of the LORD yet been revealed to him.
>
> So the LORD called Samuel again for he third time. And he arose and went to Eli and said, "Here I am, for you called me."

Then Eli discerned that the LORD was calling the boy. And Eli said to Samuel, "Go lie down, and it shall be if He calls you, that you shall say, 'Speak, LORD, for Your servant is listening.'" So Samuel went and lay down in his place.

Then the LORD came and stood and called as at other times, "Samuel! Samuel!" And Samuel said, "Speak, for Your servant is listening." (1 Sam. 3:1–10)

As the first verse reveals, "word from the LORD was rare in these days." Samuel had never heard the voice of the Lord, and therefore didn't know what it sounded like. It was only after Eli finally grasped what was happening and instructed him that Samuel was actually *expecting* to hear the Lord's voice. And as a result, that's exactly what he heard: "The LORD said to Samuel" (3:11).

Many of us are like the uninstructed Samuel in that we don't really expect to hear the Lord's voice. Perhaps you're among those who've been told that since the completion of the Bible, God no longer speaks. You're under the impression that the only way to hear God is through reading the Bible. While it's certainly true that God speaks through His written Word, His ability to speak to you isn't limited to that.

Listen to what Jesus says about this:

But I tell you the truth, it is to your advantage that I go away; for if I do not go away, the Helper will not come to you; but if I go, I will send Him to you. (John 16:7)

But when He, the Spirit of truth, comes, He will guide you into all the truth; for He will not speak on His own initiative, but whatever He hears, He will speak; and He will disclose to you what is to come. (John 16:13)

And Paul wrote this:

For all who are being led by the Spirit of God, these are sons of God. For you have not received a spirit of slavery leading to fear again, but you have received a spirit of adoption as sons by which we cry out, "Abba! Father!" The Spirit Himself testifies with our spirit that we are children of God. (Rom. 8:14–16)

While the Holy Spirit will never lead you in contradiction to His written Word, He can and will speak to you if you're positioned to listen.

Getting in position starts with an expectation to hear His voice. Remember, Jesus told His disciples that it would be to their advantage that He left, for when He did, the Holy Spirit would come and be with them always (John 16:7; Matt. 28:20). The Holy Spirit is a person. He's the very presence of God within you. He'll speak to you if you put yourself in a position to hear from Him, and if you expect Him to speak.

Make the Choice

The following brief episode from the life of Jesus serves as a good example of someone making a choice to get in position to listen:

Now as they were traveling along, He entered a village; and a woman named Martha welcomed Him into her home. She had a sister called Mary, who was seated at the Lord's feet, listening to His word. But Martha was distracted with all her preparations; and she came up to Him

and said, "Lord, do You not care that my sister has left me
to do all the serving alone? Then tell her to help me."

But the Lord answered and said to her, "Martha, Martha,
you are worried and bothered about so many things; but
only one thing is necessary, for Mary has chosen the good
part, which shall not be taken away from her." (Luke
10:38–42)

Jesus had a special relationship with Martha and Mary and their brother
Lazarus. On this particular occasion, He stopped off at their home while on
His way to Jerusalem. In just a few short verses, we get a very clear picture
of what unfolds.

Mary took a seat at the feet of Jesus, where she was perfectly positioned
to hear His every word. Martha, on the other hand, wanting to be a gracious
hostess, went into serving mode. The result: Mary heard His every word,
while Martha was in and out, catching only bits and pieces of what He said.

It didn't take long for Martha to feel she was getting the short end of
the stick. When she pulled Jesus aside to express her thoughts and feelings,
Jesus affirmed the choice Mary had made—no doubt to the surprise of
Martha, who was doing exactly what was expected of her. Women back
then weren't supposed to be seated with the men in the main room; their
place was in the kitchen. Martha was doing the "proper" thing, while Mary
apparently didn't care about what was proper.

With her Lord in her home, Mary put her full attention on Him and
made the unexpected choice to seat herself at His feet. The result: Mary
heard the word of the Lord that day, while Martha was distracted.

Getting in position to hear God speak requires a choice. You have to
choose who or what you're going to give your attention to. Obviously, there's
no shortage of attention grabbers—work, family, recreation, exercise, cell

phone, computer, newspaper, books, to-do list, email, checkbook, friends, church, "serving the Lord," a hobby, school—and the list goes on. To get yourself in a position to hear God speak, you'll need to shut out all the other voices calling for your attention.

This isn't easy to do. The other voices can be really loud, and so many of them are calling constantly.

Your response to these other voices has a great deal to do with fulfilling your responsibilities in life. In some cases, we feel we just don't seem to have time to simply sit at Jesus' feet and listen. Yet if we want to hear the Lord speak, we need to get in a position to hear. God won't compete for your attention, nor will He shout to get it. He's calling you to a relationship with Himself, a relationship based on communication—talking and listening. He wants to help guide you in all of life, but He can't if you don't stop to listen for direction.

The implications of failing to listen are significant. Take note of the condition of Martha's heart and mind in this brief episode as a result of her being distracted from the presence of Jesus:

- self-pity: "Lord, do You not care?"
- a judgmental attitude: "My sister has left me to do all the serving alone."
- a controlling urge: "Tell her to help me."
- frustration and anxiety—as Jesus pointed out: "Martha, Martha, you are worried and bothered about so many things."

If all this weren't bad enough, it's also true that Martha missed out on the blessing that would have come from being at the feet of Jesus, listening to what He had to say.

Perhaps you can identify with Martha's condition. Much is at stake based on the choices you make concerning the focus of your attention. Therefore, choose carefully.

Getting Direction

God wants to speak to you. He wants to lead you and guide you in the way you're to go.

This truth is repeated over and over again throughout the pages of the Bible. For example:

> Call to Me and I will answer you, and I will tell you great and mighty things, which you do not know. (Jer. 33:3)

> Trust in the LORD with all your heart and do not lean on your own understanding. In all your ways acknowledge Him, and He will make your paths straight. (Prov. 3:5–6)

> For all who are being led by the Spirit of God, these are sons of God. (Rom. 8:14)

Perhaps you're wondering how to receive His guidance and leading once you're in position to hear. The simple answer: *Ask Him.*

I like to ask for it this way: "Father, what am I to do about _____?" Then fill in the blank. Maybe it's a relational matter you're confused about. Maybe it's a decision you're facing regarding the future, or a monetary matter, or a health dilemma that even has your doctor confused. Perhaps there's a work matter that needs to be resolved. It may be a trial you're currently experiencing, not knowing how to proceed. Whatever it is, ask Him: "Father, what am I to do about _____?"

I think this is exactly what Paul did in his personally burdensome situation that he speaks about in 2 Corinthians 12.

> There was given me a thorn in the flesh, a messenger of Satan to torment me—to keep me from exalting myself!

Concerning this *I implored the Lord three times* that it might leave me. (12:7–8)

How did the Lord respond to those three intense entreaties from Paul to take away this "thorn in the flesh"?

And He has said to me, "My grace is sufficient for you, for power is perfected in weakness." Most gladly, therefore, I will rather boast about my weaknesses, so that the power of Christ may dwell in me. (12:9)

Six words in that passage are often overlooked—though they may be the most important words there: "And He has said to me." God *spoke* to Paul and told him His answer. Therefore Paul must have been in a position to hear Him speak to him about this matter.

This brings me to the final step in hearing God's voice—active listening.

Quiet Yourself and Listen

Give God a chance to speak. As the saying goes, "Put a cork in it and listen."

Dwight Moody wrote this:

Did it ever occur to you that if you do not hear God's answer to prayer it may be not because He is dumb but because you are deaf? Not because He has no answer to give but because you have not been listening for it? We are so busy with our service, so busy with our work, and sometimes so busy with our praying that it does not occur to us to stop our own talking and listen if God has some answer to give us with the "still small voice"; to be passive, to be quiet, to do nothing, say nothing; in some true sense think nothing—simply to be receptive and waiting for the voice.[9]

The psalmist calls this "waiting upon the Lord." Perhaps this is what God meant when He said, "Cease striving and know that I am God" (Ps. 46:10).

But we find this waiting on the Lord difficult to do.

First, we don't like to wait. We want what we want *now*. We're an instant society, accustomed to life in the fast lane. Waiting is so countercultural—in fact, counter to who we are and how we've been trained to function. Yet God calls us to "cease striving" and wait upon Him.

Second, we struggle with silence. We don't know how to handle it or what to do with it. We feel awkward in the midst of silence. We're so accustomed to the bombardment of noise. Yet God wants us to be silent so we can hear His voice.

Make a choice to get yourself in a position to hear God speak. Shut out all the other voices beckoning for you attention. Then call upon God: "Father, what am I to do about _____?"

Then listen for His answer.

How Will God Speak?

God may bring a portion of Scripture to mind that speaks into the matter you're raising. He may bring the name of a person to mind as someone to seek counsel from. He may introduce a new idea or option you hadn't previously considered. Or He may simply say, "Trust Me, walk with Me; in time I'll show you the way you're to go."

In 1 Corinthians 2:9 we read that what "God has prepared for those who love Him" includes "things which eye has not seen and ear has not heard, and which have not entered the heart of man." These are the things He wants to bring into your experience as you listen to Him.

God wants to lead you into the realm of the unexplainable because of His great love for you. The life that results from His leading is possible only through Him. He and He alone can lead you in this way. It's a life that will bring Him great glory, as the only explanation for *you* becomes *Him*.

Listen for God's voice … and let Him lead you into what He has prepared for you.

Discussion Questions

1. To what degree do you think of prayer as listening to God?
2. Using a one-to-ten scale, rate how well you actively listen to God in prayer. (1 = *I'm a lousy listener;* 10 = *I'm a great listener.*)
3. What makes it difficult for you to hear God speak?
4. What practical steps can you take in order to improve your listening skills?
5. To what degree and in what ways can you relate to Martha in Luke 10:38–42?
6. Think about the circumstances and issues you currently face in life. How would fill in this blank: "Father, what am I to do about _____?"
7. When was the last time you clearly heard God speak to you about something? Explain.

22

WALKING BY FAITH

For we walk by faith, not by sight.

2 CORINTHIANS 5:7

The Christian life is lived by faith—or at least it's supposed to be.

This is exactly what Paul states: "For we walk by faith, not by sight" (2 Cor. 5:7).

What is faith? The writer of Hebrews defines it as "the assurance of things hoped for, the conviction of things not seen" (11:1). So what does it mean to "walk by faith"—to walk in such assurance and conviction? What does this faith look like in everyday life?

In this chapter, I want to try to answer those questions. As I do, I trust you'll see that the unexplainable life is accessed by faith in God.

This truth makes total sense when you stop to consider what the writer of Hebrews says about faith a few verses later: "And without faith it is impossible to please Him, for he who comes to God must believe that He is and that He is a rewarder of those who seek Him" (11:6). It's impossible to please God apart from placing your faith in Him. God wants your life to be unexplainable apart from Him, for when this is the case, you point to Him. This kind of life cannot be achieved apart from living by faith. It's when you walk by faith that your life becomes unexplainable. Faith in everyday life will make you unexplainable apart from God.

Nine Glimpses of Faith

I want to give you nine glimpses of this faith in action—nine examples of what it means to walk by faith. I trust you'll see just how unexplainable this becomes in our world today.

• *Being joyful in the midst of trials*

Faith is choosing to live with joy in the midst of a trial, believing that God will accomplish His purposes through that trial, for His glory and your ultimate good. It takes no faith to complain and wallow in self-pity. To complain and fall prey to self-pity as a result of hardship is expected, common, normal, understandable—completely explainable. We see someone in the midst of hardship and the effect it's having on them, and we think, *I can understand and appreciate their struggle; look at what they're facing.* We expect to encounter self-pity. We don't fault or criticize such a person; that's what hard times do to people. This explains why it's so unexplainable when we encounter someone who possesses joy, only to learn later that they're in the midst of hardship. Such joy is unexpected, uncommon, abnormal. Seeing it, we think, *How can this be? How are they able to possess joy at a time like this?*

The answer: They're walking by faith. They're choosing to believe (they have faith) that God has a plan and a purpose that will be accomplished through their hardship. They believe God will eventually be glorified, and that their ultimate good will be achieved in time. This is what it means to walk by faith in the midst of a trial. Possessing joy and confidence at such a time is unexplainable apart from God.

• *Choosing to forgive*

Faith is choosing to forgive someone who has wronged you, as you release them to God, believing that He will deal with them in their best interest and yours as well. It takes no faith to be bitter and resentful. To reflect hurt and hold a grudge as a result of being wronged is completely expected, common, normal, understandable—explainable. This is what we expect to see and hear from someone who has been violated in some way.

This explains why it's so unexplainable to encounter someone we know has been violated, yet shows no marks of lingering hurt. Such a condition is unexpected, uncommon, and clearly outside the bounds of normal.

So we inquire: *How have you been able to move on as you have?*

The answer: I made a decision to forgive that person, just as God has forgiven me. I've released them to God. I believe (I have faith) that God understands what occurred, and I believe that He'll deal with them according to His purposes in their life. He knows what's best for them and what's best for me. I've brought my hurt to God, and He's healing me.

This is what it means to walk by faith when you've been wronged. Such a response is unexplainable apart from God.

• *Submitting to unreasonable authority*

Faith is submitting from the heart to a boss who's demanding, and at times unreasonable, believing that such submission finds favor with God. It takes no faith to gossip about or slander that boss or to quit that job. To talk behind the back of someone who's difficult to work for is common, normal, almost expected, and certainly explainable. This is what almost everyone does under such circumstances. We expect such an employee to move on to another job as soon as possible. That's an explainable course of events.

This is a matter Peter addresses:

> Servants, be submissive to your masters with all respect,
> not only to those who are good and gentle, but also to
> those who are unreasonable. For this finds favor, if for the
> sake of conscience toward God a person bears up under
> sorrows when suffering unjustly. For what credit is there
> if, when you sin and are harshly treated, you endure it
> with patience? But if when you do what is right and suffer
> for it you patiently endure it, this finds favor with God.
> (1 Peter 2:18–20).

The person who walks by faith understands that the favor of God is achieved by submitting respectfully to their unreasonable boss. To see someone submitting from the heart to a difficult boss—no gossip, no slander, no threat to quit, just working with all their heart—is uncommon and unexpected. It's this kind of attitude and behavior that causes others to ask, "How do you do it?" It's here that such a person can point to God's influence over them.

This is what it means to walk by faith in a difficult employment situation. Such a response is unexplainable apart from God's influence in that employee's life.

• *Giving abundantly*

Faith is giving of your financial resources beyond what's easy or comfortable, believing that God loves and honors a cheerful and generous giver. It takes no faith to give from our excess—from the money that's "left over."

Jesus tells us about this very thing:

> And He sat down opposite the treasury, and began observ-
> ing how the people were putting money into the treasury;

and many rich people were putting in large sums. A poor
widow came and put in two small copper coins, which
amount to a cent. Calling His disciples to Him, He said
to them, "Truly I say to you, this poor widow put in more
than all the contributors to the treasury; for they all put in
out of their surplus, but she, out of her poverty, put in all
she owned, all she had to live on." (Mark 12:41–44)

God is impressed not by the amount of the gift, but by the amount of
faith the gift required.

Large financial gifts—given from excess and requiring no faith—are
really quite common in our world. Such generosity is on display regularly.
On the other hand, generosity that displays faith in God, like that of the
widow in Mark 12, is so very uncommon, unexpected, abnormal, and
unexplainable apart from God.

This is what it means to walk by faith in terms of giving. Furthermore,
when a person's lifestyle reflects frugality toward self and generosity toward
others—which should be the case, according to the Bible—the opportunity
to point to God's influence is clearly present.

• *Loving the unlovable*

Faith is choosing to love a person who's difficult to love, believing that
God honors those who obey the command to "love your neighbor as yourself." It takes no faith to walk away from unlovable people. Some people seem
almost impossible to love—or even to like. For any number of reasons, they're
just plain difficult to deal with. In fact, it's just easier to avoid them; not deal
with them at all. Yet God calls us to love others, even the unlovable.

The example of Jesus in this regard is powerful. He reached out to the
outcasts—lepers, tax collectors, prostitutes, the poor, the lame—the list
goes on. Those who were forgotten … He remembered. For us to do the

same is an act of faith, as we need to depend upon God to pour His love for such people through our hearts.

If we depend solely upon our own capacity to love in such cases, our love will prove insufficient. The display of undeserved and unconditional love toward a hard-to-love person is uncommon, unexpected, and unexplainable apart from God. This is what it means to walk by faith in terms of dealing with hard-to-love people.

• *Acting with integrity*

Faith is acting with complete integrity in a business transaction, believing that God can make up for any lost profit that might result. It takes no faith to lie, cheat, or compromise. To fudge on quality, to tell a white lie, or to fail to disclose the whole truth is common practice when profit is on the line.

Such actions have plenty of attempted justifications: "Everybody's doing it"; "I wouldn't be able to compete otherwise"; "It's just a trick of the trade"; "Ultimately, it's not my fault." Integrity is really attractive—until achieving it results in a loss of profit.

Faith is believing that God honors integrity. To walk by faith is to act with complete and total integrity, in spite of the implications, believing that God will honor you for doing so.

Such integrity is rare to find in the marketplace today. It's certainly the exception, not the rule.

For the Christian, the temptation to compromise for the sake of profit is seen as a test of character, while it's perhaps even more a test of faith. And to have victory over such temptation is uncommon, unexpected, unusual—unexplainable apart from faith in God.

• *Persevering in prayer*

Faith is perseverance in prayer in spite of God's seeming silence or inactivity, believing that in His time and in His way, He'll answer. It takes no faith to quit praying and conclude that God doesn't answer prayer. Discouragement in prayer is certainly a common feeling. We've all been there. It's very typical to quit praying about a request that's gone unanswered for quite some time. Perhaps this is why it's so inspiring to meet someone who has been praying the same request for many years, perhaps many decades, though the request remains unanswered.

Such perseverance in prayer is uncommon and unusual, and points to a deep and abiding faith in God. This is the kind of faith that points others to God and encourages them to persevere in prayer.

• *Going boldly where God leads*

Faith is following a clear leading from God to make a life-altering decision—even with an uncertain outcome—believing that God honors faith-filled obedience. It takes no faith to live within the confines of personal control and comfort. And let's be honest: We all like to be in control over the affairs of our life. This is where we feel most comfortable. Therefore, to follow a leading that shifts control from us to God can be rather disconcerting. Depending upon God is certainly easier to talk about than to do.

But the Bible is filled with stories of people who followed the leading of God into unchartered waters. Hebrews 11, "the faith chapter," identifies a whole host of people who responded to the call of God to venture out from the confines of personal control and comfort to a place of true dependence upon God.

If you choose to walk by faith, there's no doubt that God will call you from time to time to leave the safe haven of personal control and comfort and make a move that requires you to depend upon Him. In some cases, such faith will provide an opportunity to say, "It is God who led me here." In other cases, the step of faith you took wasn't seen by others, but the results of doing so are.

These results can only be explained by God's involvement. Either way, acting in faith in response to a leading from God eventually points back to God.

• *Denying the flesh*

Faith is choosing to deny the desires of your flesh, believing that there's greater reward in pleasing God than there is in pleasing your flesh. It takes no faith to indulge in fleshly pleasures. The writer of Hebrews helps us understand this:

> By faith Moses, when he had grown up, refused to be called the son of Pharaoh's daughter, choosing rather to endure ill-treatment with the people of God than to enjoy the passing pleasures of sin, considering the reproach of Christ greater riches than the treasures of Egypt; for he was looking to the reward. (Heb. 11:24–26)

To do what "feels good"—to "enjoy the passing pleasures of sin"—is common, expected, and very normal in our world today. On the other hand, to submit one's pleasures to the will of God is unusual, unexpected, and not at all common. Personal discipline, self-restraint, and doing what is right in spite of one's feelings is so uncommon that we take note when we see it.

Profile of Faith

As you can see from the brief list I've put together, it takes a great deal of faith to live a life that honors God. And my list only scratches the surface. There are so many other ways in which faith touches daily life.

I trust you can also see just how rare, how uncommon, how unusual, how unexplainable is the person who walks by faith. When you add up what this person looks like simply based on the examples I've given, here's a composite profile:

- The ability to experience joy in the midst of hardship.
- The capacity to forgive when wronged and to express mercy and grace in response.
- The humility to respectfully submit to leadership that is harsh, demanding, and perhaps altogether unreasonable.
- The display of generosity that reveals that God and others are your true treasure.
- The love to embrace those that most others have turned away from.
- The integrity of word and deed that won't be compromised in spite of personal loss.
- The perseverance to overcome discouragement, no matter how great it becomes.
- A desire to obey God that surpasses the desire for personal control and comfort.
- The discipline and self-control to do what's right in the eyes of God, in spite of what you feel like doing.

Now let me ask: Is the person I just profiled common in your experience? Do you run across such people on a regular basis? Or would you say that such a person is so uncommon, so unusual, so radical, that encountering such a person immediately calls for further explanation?

This is what it means to be unexplainable apart from God. Walking by faith will make you such a person. God will be honored, and others will see Him in you.

Discussion Questions

1. Can you recall a time when you had to walk by faith? Explain how this came about, and what happened.

2. This chapter offers nine glimpses of what walking by faith looks like in everyday life. Can you relate to any of these at this time in your life? Are there any additional ways in which you currently need to walk by faith? Explain.

3. To what degree does the biblical truth of "walking by faith" characterize your daily life? (Answer *not at all, somewhat,* or *totally.*)

23

THE GRACE TO BE UNEXPLAINABLE

My grace is sufficient for you.

2 CORINTHIANS 12:9

Bill Moyers' distinguished career as a journalist dates back to the 1960s, when he served as White House press secretary for President Johnson. He hosted the PBS news program *Bill Moyers Journal* during the 1970s, and was a CBS editor and analyst from 1976 through 1986. In more recent years, he has hosted several PBS series. As evidence to his success as a journalist, he has received more than thirty Emmys. While much of this you may know, what you may not know is that Bill Moyers originally had his sights set on the ministry. Having grown up in the Southern Baptist church, Moyers attended and graduated from Southwestern Baptist Theological Seminary with a master's in divinity. In a recent interview that appeared in *World* magazine, the seventy-four-year-old Moyers said this about his faith:

Someone recently asked me what the moment was when I became a Christian. And I told them, I never did become a Christian. I can't turn the other cheek. I can't sell all my possessions and give them away. I can't love my enemy. I am not a Christian because I can't do what Jesus asks. But, I care deeply about that figure. He has instructed my faith; He looms large in my life. But I can't do what He asks me to do, so I can't legitimately claim to be a Christian.

As the interviewer correctly points out about Moyers in the article's introduction, "He believes that an individual's Christianity is based on what he does, rather than what Jesus has done."

If being a Christian is based upon one's ability to do what Jesus asks, then who could claim to be a Christian? I know I couldn't; could you?

Fortunately and thankfully, this is not the case. Listen to Paul declare what God has done for us:

> He saved us, not on the basis of deeds which we have done in righteousness, but according to His mercy, by the washing of regeneration and renewing by the Holy Spirit, whom He poured out upon us richly through Jesus Christ our Savior, so that being justified by His grace we would be made heirs according to the hope of eternal life. (Titus 3:5–7)

As Paul states, we're saved not on the basis of what we have done or can do, but on the basis of what God did on our behalf.

Saved by Grace

In Ephesians 2:8–9, Paul writes, "For by grace you have been saved through faith; and that not of yourselves, it is the gift of God; not as a result of works, so that no one may boast."

Our salvation comes as a result of God's grace toward us. This grace is defined as "the unmerited favor of God." *Unmerited* means undeserved and unearned. This grace cannot be purchased at any price. It is "the gift of God."

Of course, this gift came at the highest of prices for God:

> For God so loved the world, that He gave His only begot-
> ten Son, that whoever believes in Him shall not perish,
> but have eternal life. (John 3:16)

God's grace came to us in the person of Jesus. God offered up the life of His one and only Son to pay for my sins and yours. And lest you think that this sacrifice of Jesus was God the Father's decision alone, listen to these words from Jesus Himself:

> No one has taken it away from Me, but I lay it down on
> My own initiative. I have authority to lay it down, and
> I have authority to take it up again. This commandment I
> received from My Father. (John 10:18)

What would cause God the Father to make such a sacrifice? What would motivate Jesus to offer Himself on our behalf?

In a word, *love.* "For God so *loved* the world, that He gave His only begotten Son."

While I can explain what Jesus did, I can't really explain why He did it. Sure, I can say that love motivated Him, and yes, I can recite John 3:16.

But that doesn't really explain it, does it? Who can truly understand the love of God?

I have three children, and like every other parent I know, I wouldn't give the life of any one of them for my best friend on their best day. Yet God gave *His Son* for people who beat Him, spit on Him, and called Him names as He hung on a cross shedding His blood for them. In response, Jesus said, "Father, forgive them, for they do not know what they are doing."

Can you explain that? Sacrifice and humility on that level are—well, unexplainable.

This is the grace of God. It's this grace that saves us from our sin. This grace is the gift of God. And as is the case with every gift, it is given with the hope that it will be accepted. While this sounds easy enough to grasp, for many it's not. Most of us have been taught, trained, and raised to believe that we get what we earn. We're accustomed to operating that way. And frankly, our pride likes it that way. We work for and earn what we get so we can say, "I did it."

Well, God doesn't work that way. No matter what or how much we do, we can't earn or merit His favor. Only by grace can we be saved. In this way, our very salvation is unexplainable apart from God. The only way anyone can explain their salvation and claim to be a Christian is, "God did it." This requires humility on our part and directs all the glory to God.

So what can you do in response to the grace of God? Accept it! Receive it! And embrace it as the life-changing gift that it is.

Live by Grace

God's grace doesn't stop at our salvation. It's His grace that makes it possible for us to do what Jesus asks.

Bill Moyers said, "I can't turn the other cheek. I can't sell all my possessions and give them away. I can't love my enemy. I am not a Christian because I can't do what Jesus asks." To which I say, "Join the club. Who can?" Left to ourselves, none of us can do what Jesus asks. This is where the grace of God continues to work on our behalf.

Consider the apostle Paul, who said he was given "a thorn in the flesh, a messenger of Satan to torment me—to keep me from exalting myself" (2 Cor. 12:7). While we can only speculate what this "thorn" was, we know it was so burdensome to Paul that he "implored the Lord three times that it might leave me" (12:8). Paul was saying, "I can't take it; I can't do it; it's more than I can bear; please take it from me." He was withering under the burden of this "thorn."

In response to his entreaty, God said to Paul, "My grace is sufficient for you, for power is perfected in weakness" (12:9). Paraphrased: "You're right, Paul, you can't do it; it's more than you can handle. However, I can give you what you need to continue on, for my strength is available when yours runs out."

This is the grace of God by which we live.

As a result of God's response, Paul went on to write, "Most gladly, therefore, I will rather boast about my weaknesses, so that the power of Christ may dwell in me. Therefore I am content with weaknesses, with insults, with distresses, with persecutions, with difficulties, for Christ's sake; for when I am weak, then I am strong" (12:9–10).

The only hope you and I have of being able to do what Jesus asks is the grace of God. We need God's grace to help us turn the other cheek. We need God's grace if we're going to practice generosity toward others and frugality toward self. Apart from God's grace, who of us can love our enemy and sincerely pray for those who persecute us? Apart from the grace of God, is it possible to truly be content in times of need, loss, or hardship? Without the grace of God, how will any of us faithfully steward all that God has given us for His glory?

If not for the grace of God, how will we have victory in the face of overpowering temptation? If not for the grace of God, how will we grow in love, joy, peace, patience, kindness, goodness, faithfulness, gentleness, and self-control? Unless we receive the grace of God, how will we be able to journey through life doing good? Apart from the grace of God, what do we have to offer someone who is experiencing demonic influence?

We need the grace of God to find joy in times of trial and humility in times of testing. We need God's grace in order to give ourselves to that which is beyond our own pleasure and comfort. Without the grace of God, where will we find passion to love others as God does? Where can we find the strength to do whatever we do with all our heart, as unto the Lord? How can we walk worthy of our calling, apart from the grace of God?

It's only by the grace of God that we're able to love those who are hard to love. It's only by the grace of God that we can find the strength to persevere in prayer when we're overwhelmed by discouragement. It's only by the grace of God that we're able to enter into and build a relationship with God, hear His voice, and walk by faith.

Everything I've written of in this book is made possible only by the grace of God. Only by the grace of God can we experience the peace of God, which surpasses comprehension. Only by the grace of God can we pursue and find success that lasts forever. Only by the grace of God can we experience feelings of significance apart from our performance.

Paul knew that he lived by the grace of God. In 1 Corinthians 15:10, he writes, "But by the grace of God I am what I am, and His grace toward me did not prove vain; but I labored even more than all of them, yet not I, but the grace of God with me."

Bill Moyers is right; he can't do what Jesus asks. And neither can you and I. It's only by the grace of God that we're saved, and it's only by the grace of God that we can do what Jesus asks. Even to try, apart from the grace of God, is absolutely exhausting.

This is why Jesus said, "Come to Me, all who are weary and heavy-laden, and I will give you rest" (Matt. 11:28). The religious leaders of Jesus' day had put the burden on people to try and do what God asked of them. In the end, those who tried to do so in their own strength ended up "weary and heavy-laden" and desperate for rest. This explains why Paul wrote these words in Philippians 4:13: "I can do all things through Him who strengthens me." Just as we want to be able to earn our salvation, we want to be able to do all that God asks of us. We've been raised with the goal of achieving independence. Being dependent and needing to rely on others is seen as weakness. The self-made man or woman is applauded and looked to as a role model. Again, pride likes it this way. Pride likes to say, "I did it." There's just one problem; we *can't* do it. The only way we can be who Jesus asks us to be and do what He calls us to do is the grace of God. To the degree that we fulfill any of His commands, the only explanation is, "God did it."

This is the grace of God by which we live. It is God's grace that makes it possible for us to do what is otherwise impossible. It is God's unexplainable grace that makes us unexplainable. This too requires humility on our part and directs all the glory to God.

Inasmuch as this book has been chock-full of Scripture, it's only fitting that I end up with a few Scriptures concerning God's grace:

> But He gives a greater grace. Therefore it says, "God is opposed to the proud, but gives grace to the humble." (James 4:6)

> Therefore let us draw near with confidence to the throne of grace, so that we may receive mercy and may find grace to help in time of need. (Heb. 4:16)

> And God is able to make all grace abound to you, so that always having all sufficiency in everything, you may have an abundance for every good deed. (2 Cor. 9:8)

Thanks be to God for His indescribable gift! (2 Cor. 9:15)

May God's unexplainable grace make *you* unexplainable … so that you point to Him.

Discussion Questions

1. What does Jesus ask of you that is impossible for you to do without the grace of God? Be specific.

2. For what do you need the grace of God today? Be specific.

3. What are the two or three greatest takeaways for you from your study of *Unexplainable*?

Notes

1 *Webster's Third New International Dictionary* and *The American Heritage Dictionary for Learners of English*, s.v. "Contentment."

2 From the Classis Holland Ministry News, 2005.

3 "Affluenza," produced by John de Graaf and Vivia Boe, KCTS/ Seattle and Oregon Public Broadcasting, 1998. (http://www.pbs. org/kcts/affluenza/home.html).

4 Don Cousins, *Experiencing LeaderShift* (Colorado Springs, CO: David C. Cook, 2008), 184–85.

5 Rick Warren, *The Purpose Driven Life* (Grand Rapids, MI: Zondervan, 2002), 17.

6 John Beckett, *Loving Monday* (Downer's Grove, IL: InterVarsity Press, 1998), 125.

7 Mark Sanborn, *The Fred Factor* (New York: Broadway Business, 2004), 3–5.

8 Beckett, *Loving Monday*, 151.

9 Dwight Moody, *Thoughts for the Quiet Hour* (Chicago: Fleming H. Revell Company, 1900).

Unexplainable for Small Groups

The message of *Unexplainable* will have its strongest impact when this book is used in small groups for study and discussion. To that end, a companion DVD is available that reinforces and deepens this book's content.

An eight-week study course is recommended, with the chapters grouped in the following weekly structure (use the discussion questions that are included at the end of each chapter):

Session One

Chapter 1: Unexplainable … Apart from God

Session Two

Chapter 2: So Desired, Yet So Elusive

Chapter 3: Contentment's First Secret: *Rejoice in the Lord*

Chapter 4: Contentment's Second Secret: *Pray about Everything*

Session Three

Chapter 5: Contentment's Third Secret: *Celebrate Thanksgiving Every Day*

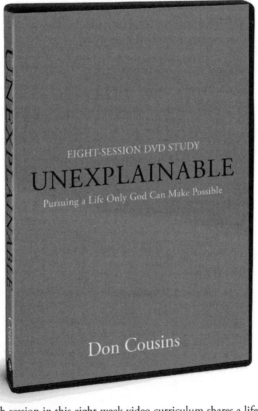

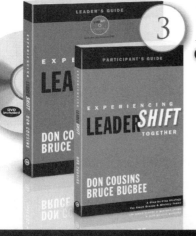